A Software Engineer Learns HTML5, JavaScript & jQuery

DANE CAMERON

CONTENTS

PREFACE

JavaScript (and its frameworks such as jQuery) and HTML (along with its style sheet language CSS) have become a ubiquitous presence in software development. Due to their monopoly position in web browsers, and the fact web browsers have spread from PCs to phones, tablets and TVs; this pervasiveness will continue to grow and grow.

Despite their success, many software engineers are apprehensive about JavaScript and HTML. This apprehensiveness is not completely unfounded; both JavaScript and HTML were rushed in their early years, and driven by commercial rather than engineering interests. As a result, many dubious features crept into these languages. Due to backwards compatibility concerns, most of these features still remain.

In addition, many software engineers have used these languages without ever learning them. JavaScript and HTML have low barriers to entry, and this, along with their similarity to other languages, led many software engineers to conclude that there really was nothing much to learn.

If you have not used JavaScript and HTML for a number of years you may be surprised at what they now offer. Browser based web applications are now capable of matching or exceeding the sophistication and scale of traditional desktop applications. In order to create complex web applications however, it is essential to learn these languages.

This book takes the point of view that once you have a strong grasp of the fundamentals, the details will take care of themselves. It will not present you with long lists of APIs, or intricate details of every attribute, these can be found in reference manuals. It will focus on the details of each language that are fundamental to understanding how they work.

I hope this book helps you discover the elegance and beauty of JavaScript and HTML, and makes you think differently about what can be achieved with these languages.

October, 2013

1 INTRODUCTION

I'm not going to second guess your motivations for reading this book – but I would like to tell you how I arrived at writing it.

I was a software engineer with 15 years' experience writing large-scale enterprise Java applications. Typically these applications performed system integration functions, rather than end-user functionality.

I then joined a team writing a complex web application from scratch. This web application had a number of requirements I had not encountered before:

- It had to run inside the latest version of all major browsers.

- It had to be capable of running without network connectivity for periods of time, and therefore needed to store reasonably large amounts of data on the client.

- It had to be capable of reading files selected by the user while offline.

- It needed to be highly dynamic, and allow complex interactions without page refreshes.

- It needed to perform as well or better than a desktop application.

- It needed to be standards based, and not utilize browser plugins.

I had written simple HTML pages and simple JavaScript over the years but was often frustrated by it. JavaScript was particularly frustrating: it resembled Java (which I knew well), but it seemed to have got many things wrong. The more I tried to apply my Java thinking to JavaScript, the worse things seemed to get.

I did at least realize that I had not taken the time to learn JavaScript. I had made many assumptions about what JavaScript was, and how it worked, but I had never taken the time to verify these assumptions.

Before starting my new project I decided to start from scratch and learn the best approached for building a web application with the languages available. I had used enough web applications over recent years to know the potential browser-based technologies offered, but I didn't know the best way to unlock this potential.

The more I learned about the platform modern browsers offered software engineers the more surprised I became. The standards loosely grouped together as HTML5 offer a wide-ranging set of features from data storage to offline resource storage to file management.

In addition, the more I learned about JavaScript the more impressed I became. JavaScript may bear a superficial similarity to Java, but in actuality it has more in common with functional languages such as LISP and Scheme. The features that had initially troubled me about JavaScript turned out to be enormous strengths in the language.

Finally, I came across the jQuery library. jQuery does not allow a software engineer to do anything that could not be done with native JavaScript APIs, but it provides such an elegant abstraction on top of JavaScript that it became an essential component in my toolbox. It removed my final hesitation with browser-based technologies: the cumbersome DOM API.

This book is the book I wanted to read at the beginning of my journey. It starts from the assumption that you have some training as a software engineer or computer programmer, and presents the essentials you need to understand, without attempting to cover all aspects of each language. Once these fundamentals are understood, the process of expanding your knowledge with these languages is comparatively trivial.

Before beginning, it is worth reviewing the rise of HTML and JavaScript over the last few years in-particular, and the reasons this has happened.

Browser Wars Part 2

The original browser wars took place in the late 1990s between Netscape and Microsoft. Microsoft won. As a result, browser technology stagnated: from 2001-2006 the user experience barely progressed at all.

The second browser war started around 2005, first with Firefox, and then with the rise of Chrome. This browser war became an arms race as all major browser vendors added new and interesting features to their browsers. Many of these features were eventually standardized as part of the HTML5 standardization process, and adopted by other browser vendors.

One of the main consequences of the second browser war was a dramatic improvement in the performance of JavaScript.

JavaScript is an interpreted language. As such it tends to have worse performance than a compiled language such as C or C++. This is because an intermediary (the interpreter) is responsible for taking instructions, and converting them to machine specific instructions in real time as the program executes. The performance of JavaScript was so poor in Internet Explorer it was really only appropriate for simple tasks such as form validation.

Google in particular recognized that the performance of JavaScript was a major hindrance to the development of web applications. In order to improve the performance of JavaScript, Google developed the V8 JavaScript engine in 2008.

The V8 JavaScript engine produced massive increases in JavaScript performance by compiling JavaScript into machine language on a Just-In-Time (JIT) basis rather than interpreting it as it was executed.

Since the release of V8, all major browser vendors have implemented JIT compilation in their JavaScript engines. Browser vendors also began to actively compete amongst one another to create the fastest JavaScript engine, and a variety of benchmarks have been created to compare their relative performance. Microsoft finally entered the race with IE9, and continued to build on their performance with IE10.

JavaScript has now reached the stage where performance is seldom a major issue, and the performance of large scale web applications can equal or surpass that of desktop applications. All major browsers have highly optimized JavaScript engines, and the performance has reached the point where JavaScript has begun to be used outside the browser: Node.js successfully uses JavaScript as a server side technology (using the V8 JavaScript engine).

Rise of the Web Application

As a result of the improvements in browser technologies, it has become possible to create complex web applications that run entirely within browsers.

In the early days of the World Wide Web, pages were largely static in their content. Web sites quickly evolved to allow dynamic interaction with users, and this led to the possibility of commerce web sites such as Amazon. The set of technologies adopted to allow the dynamic manipulation of web pages was referred to as DHTML (Dynamic HTML), and is really the precursor to the HTML5 technologies explored in this book.

DHTML allowed web pages to be manipulated in real time after they were loaded, but it was still difficult to create large-scale web applications that did not rely on page refreshes to perform most of their actions, largely due to the performance issues with JavaScript, and the lack of browser APIs for relatively simple features, such as data-storage.

The first major game changer was Gmail, which was released to the general public in 2007. Not only did Gmail accelerate the trend towards cloud computing by offering users an unprecedented 1GB of storage, it popularized the use of AJAX.

AJAX allows a web page to interact with a web server after the page is loaded, and without requiring a refresh of the web page. This meant a web application could consist of a single web page that would redraw itself as the user interacted with it, and as it received additional data from the server.

Google didn't invent the technologies behind AJAX (in fact Microsoft did), and they weren't the first to use AJAX to develop a web application, but they brought AJAX into the limelight, and showed programmers what could be achieved.

AJAX has become such a dominant technology in the last 5 years it is hard to conceive of a time when it did not exist.

Once people realized what could be achieved inside the browser, there came a push from both IT departments and end-users to use browser based web applications for a variety of tasks that had once been the domain of desktop applications. Browser based web applications provide many benefits to their users:

- There is no need to install the application on each machine.

- New versions of software can be released on a regular basis without needing users to follow an upgrade process. In fact some web applications have daily releases of software.

- Web applications can be hosted on cloud based infrastructure, leading to higher availability, and lower costs.

- The same web application can be used on multiple devices, including handheld devices such as phones and tablets.

- Users can access the application from anywhere in the world at any time of the day or night.

Web browsers have now become akin to operating systems in the features and libraries they offer software engineers. It now makes sense to think of the browser as a mature platform for software development, just as you may think of OSX, Android or Windows as a platform.

The Networked World

The other major change that has occurred in the last 5 years is the ubiquitous availability of high-speed networks. Many people now have near-permanent access to high-speed networks, either wired or wireless.

The availability of networks has led to the rise of cloud computing. Cloud computing is an umbrella term for a number of technologies, but at heart it means that software engineers do not need to think about hardware, hardware is provided as a service.

For users, cloud computing means their applications and data are available at any time, and from any location.

Cloud computing is one of the fastest growing trends in IT, and is only set to grow further and faster as more and more devices become network enabled. It is estimated in 2013 that half of Americans own 3 or more network enabled devices.

Although it is possible to write cloud based applications that do not run inside browsers, browsers are the perfect platform for cloud based applications, because the one constant all devices have in common is a web browser, therefore a single version of the application can be written that runs on all platforms.

Conclusion

The conclusion you can draw from this chapter is that HTML5 and JavaScript are perfectly placed to be the driving force powering the applications most users interact with on a daily basis.

2 ABOUT THIS BOOK

What you need

This book assumes you have some experience developing software, and preferably have at least a basic understanding of HTML.

This book will not offer step-by-step tutorials on the basics of either HTML or JavaScript. Even with no prior experience with these languages however, the process of writing a web application will introduce you to all the essential aspects of these languages, just not necessarily in the same order a traditional tutorial would.

If you have not encountered JavaScript and/or HTML previously it may be advisable to gain an understanding of the basic syntax of these languages (loops, conditional expressions etc.) before beginning. Websites such as http://www.w3schools.com provide basic introductions to both HTML and JavaScript.

The exercises in this book can be performed on any computer with access to the following:

1. A text editor for writing code. Notepad++ (http://notepad-plus-plus.org) is a good option for Windows, Text Wrangler (http://www.barebones.com/products/textwrangler) is a good choice for Macs, and EMacs is a good choice for Linux. You may also choose to use an Integrated Development Environment (IDE) such as Eclipse.

2. Chrome or Firefox web browser. If you choose to use Firefox, you will need to install the Firebug plugin to gain access to a full suite of development tools. The examples and screenshots in this book will use Chrome, but there is nothing presented in this book that does not work with Firefox, IE10 or Safari. I believe the developer tools in Chrome are now superior to those offered by other browsers, therefore if you are starting from scratch I strongly recommend Chrome.

3. A Web Server. This will only be required later in the book, and there is a chapter explaining how to install and use the Mongoose web server. You may choose to use any other web server you like, but the instructions will only be provided for Mongoose.

All the examples in this book are accessible from the following web site:

www.cisdal.com/publishing.html

A zip file is provided for each chapter of the book (where appropriate) containing the resources for the web application as they stand at the end of the chapter.

As mentioned above, this book will guide you through the process of developing a web application. Throughout the first half of this book the web application can be served directly from your local file-system rather than a web server.

All web browsers can display HTML files directly from the file-system: you can simply drag and drop the HTML file into the web browser, or use the File -> Open File option from the browser menu bar.

Unfortunately, browsers will often cache resources such as JavaScript and CSS files when a web page is loaded directly from the file-system. In order to circumvent this in Chrome you can opt to open a new window in Incognito mode:

Any resources loaded by the browser in this mode will not be cached.

If this proves too painful, you can choose to serve pages from a local web server from the start of this book. Chapter 8 provides detailed instructions for installing the Mongoose web server on your computer. Pages served through a web server can still be cached by the web browser, but using "force refresh" will reliably ensure the resources are refreshed:

- Command+Shift+r on OSX

- Ctrl+F5 on Windows

Many of the examples in this book, particularly in the early chapters, can be run directly using a JavaScript interpreter. All major browsers now provide development tools offering direct access to a JavaScript interpreter.

In order to access the Chrome interpreter, simply open Chrome, and type:

- Command+Option+i on OSX

- F12 or Ctrl+Shift+I on Windows

Alternatively, you can right click anywhere on any web page and choose "Inspect Element":

```
Back
Forward
Reload

Save As...
Print...
View Page Source
View Page Info

Inspect Element
```

Once the Developer Tools are open, click the "Console" tab.

In order to prove that this is a genuine JavaScript interpreter, simply type 1+1 at the command prompt:

```
×   Elements  Resources  Network  Sources  Timeline  Profiles  Audits | Console |
>  1+1
   2
>
```

One aspect of browsers that have advanced tremendously over the last few years are the tools offered to developers. Browser vendors have realized that there is a direct benefit to them when developers use their browsers, and therefore actively woo developers with the tools they offer. This book will introduce you to many of the features offered by the Chrome developer tools, but it is worth investigating the various capabilities on your own.

Conventions

Code in this book will utilize the following font:

`This is code`

When code is executed inside the JavaScript interpreter, the input will be prefixed with a ">" character: when entering these commands yourself this should be omitted. In addition an empty line will separate input from output:

```
> 1+1

2
```

If two commands are shown simultaneously, these will be separated by an additional empty line between the result of the first command and the input of the second command:

```
>1+1


2


>2+2


4
```

If the output is irrelevant to the point being made, it may be omitted.

Feedback

I would love to hear your feedback (positive and negative) on this book. Please email me at dane@cisdal.com.

3 A BRIEF OVERVIEW OF WEB APPLICATIONS

This book is designed to teach you how to write rich web applications utilizing the tools and technologies available natively in web browsers (as opposed to plugins). This book will focus solely on the languages and libraries available in the latest versions of the following web browsers:

- Chrome

- Firefox

- IE

- Safari

- Opera

Many of the examples in this book will not work in older browsers, and in many cases there are no workarounds. When writing a web application the obvious first question to ask is "What browsers, and which versions of those browsers do I need or want to support?"

There is an obvious trade-off involved:

- The more browser and browser versions you support, the more users can use your web application. Remember, some users, particularly in corporate environments, do not choose either their browser or their browser version.

- The more browser and browser versions you support, the more restrictions you will encounter in terms of availability and compatibility of APIs. Later in this book we will encounter an approach called polyfills that allow you to "upgrade" the features offered by a user's browser, but this approach will not always work.

All major browsers now support auto updates. Although this feature can be turned off, it does mean that it is no longer a wild assumption to assume that most users will have the latest version of their favorite browser, at least outside corporate environments.

The main exception to this is Internet Explorer. Internet Explorer 10 and 11 is not available on older versions of Windows; therefore many users will have older versions of Internet Explorer. In general, most of the examples in this book will work in Internet Explorer 9, some will work in

Internet Explorer 8, but supporting Internet Explorer 6 and 7 becomes a more daunting proposition.

The web site http://caniuse.com is an invaluable resource for understanding the features offered by various browsers and browser versions.

What is a web application?

A reasonable question to ask is "What is a web application, and how is it different from a web site?" Even the opening section of the HTML5 specification states that it is designed to address "...the vague subject referred to as web applications".

There is no definitive answer to this question, but the web application developed in this book exhibits the following characteristics:

- It uses a web browser for its user interface.

- It allows users to perform actions and manipulate data without performing screen refreshes.

- It is interactive, and responds promptly to user actions.

- It stores data on behalf of a user, either on the client or the server.

- If it needs to access a web server, it does so using asynchronous AJAX calls.

- It favors asynchronous APIs over synchronous APIs.

- It may be available even when the user is not connected to the Internet.

It will be important throughout this book that you understand the difference between an asynchronous and a synchronous API. Although this book will offer many examples, the basic difference between the two is:

- A synchronous API waits for a response, and blocks everything else from happening in the application until that response is received.

- An asynchronous API does not wait for a response, but instead asks to be notified when a response is available. As a result it does not block other functionality in the application from progressing.

The HTML5 specification suggests that web applications will also exhibit the following features:

- They are used on an occasional basis, or on a regular basis but from different locations.

- They have low CPU requirements.

There is some truth to these statements. For instance, a web application version of a word processor will not generally exhibit the same usability and features as a native word processor, but has considerable advantages if documents need to be edited by many different people in different locations.

This chapter will briefly introduce you to the languages that we will use to develop the web application throughout this book.

HTML5

HTML5 can be a confusing term.

HTML5 includes a specification of a markup language for creating documents that can be rendered in web browsers. As a markup language, HTML5 both extends and rationalizes earlier versions of HTML and XHTML.

As part of its extension of HTML, HTML5 offers a new set of tags to web site developers. Many of these tags are designed to provide greater descriptive power to HTML. For instance, HTML5 contains **header** and **footer** tags. These tags do not allow pages to do anything or look any different than they did previously, and are one of the less interesting aspects of HTML5; we will examine a subset of these new tags in this book.

HTML5 also contains new tags to support audio and video, and a canvas for rendering 2D shapes and bitmaps. It is these features of HTML5 that have drawn a lot of attention, particularly the way these features position HTML5 as a direct competitor to Adobe Flash. Apple refuses to allow Adobe Flash on certain devices, arguing that websites should use HTML5 equivalents, since they are standards compliant, and do not require plugins. This book will largely ignore the multimedia aspects of HTML5, since they are usually not relevant for web applications, but it is important to know they are there.

As part of its rationalization of XHTML in particular, HTML5 acknowledges that the strictness enforced by earlier versions of the HTML standards was both unnecessary (browsers still rendered pages that broke the rules), and counter-productive (since there was no standard for how browsers should handle pages that were invalid in some way, it was left up to each vendor). The HTML5 specification contains detailed rules for how browser vendors should create a consistent Document Object Model from the input provided. A large part of the HTML5 specification deals directly with these rules, and again, is beyond the scope of this book.

 Don't worry if you are not familiar with the Document Object Model (it will be explained below) or XHTML (it is largely obsolete).

HTML5 also enhances the form components available in HTML. In addition to providing new types of input fields (such as date pickers and color pickers), HTML5 provides additional attributes on existing input fields. HTML5 also provides native validation of form components.

In addition to providing a markup language and a set of form components, HTML5 is a set of standards for APIs that web browsers can implement. These APIs are wide ranging and varied, and range from offline storage of data and content, reading files, background processes, server-sent events and much more. It is these features of HTML5 that are truly turning the web browser into a platform for application development. This book will use many of the new APIs when developing the example web application.

The HTML5 standards process is interesting in its own right. Many of the standards are actually reverse engineered from features already present in web browsers. For instance, the technology behind AJAX (the XMLHttpRequest object) was first developed as a proprietary feature of Internet Explorer. Other browsers then reverse engineered this feature, and finally, once the major browsers supported it, it was standardized by W3C (in fact, it is still a working draft).

The World Wide Web Consortium (W3C) is the main standards organization for the World Wide Web. Their web site can be found here: http://www.w3.org while the HTML5 specification can be found here http://www.w3.org/TR/html5

The HTML5 specification is actually produced by two separate bodies: W3C and WHATWG. Both bodies offer the standards under their own licenses. WHATWG actually deserve far more credit than W3C for HTML5, W3C initially voted not to be involved with HTML5, but to continue pushing XML based standards. W3C finally acknowledged they had backed the wrong horse and became actively involved with HTML5.

It is also worth mentioning that the W3C and WHATWG versions of the specifications are not identical. From a software engineers point of view this is largely irrelevant. Web designers have a saying "code always wins". This is also true of HTML5: the specification is largely irrelevant; it is the browser implementations that matter.

In some cases, one particular browser vendor drives a standard. This occasionally leads to an impasse, as has occurred with the Web SQL API. In other cases a speciation is progressed that is not widely supported (such as the File Writer and File System API), and therefore has an uncertain future. In the best cases however, all major browser support the API according to the standard agreed.

The other important aspect of HTML5 is that it is a living standard. As you will see in the following chapters, the HTML5 document type does not specify a version: it is just HTML, and it will change as the standards progress, and as browsers adopt those standards.

JavaScript

JavaScript is the only language natively supported in virtually all web browsers in existence. JavaScript first appeared in 1995 in an early version of the Netscape Navigator browser, and quickly migrated to Internet Explorer. JavaScript is essential for adding dynamic and interactive features to a web application.

Although Microsoft continues to support VBScript, this has not been implemented in other browsers meaning it is not a viable option when creating Web Applications.

It is worth clearing up a small point regarding terminology first. JavaScript has been formalized in the ECMAScript language specification. When this book refers to JavaScript, technically it is referring to ECMAScript version 5.

JavaScript was named after the programming language Java, but this was primarily to allow JavaScript to piggyback off the name recognition of Java rather than any intrinsic similarity between the languages. JavaScript is in fact a very different language from Java, specifically:

- JavaScript supports dynamic typing as opposed to Java, which supports static typing. This means you can declare a variable in JavaScript without declaring its type, which will only be derived at run-time.

- JavaScript has first class functions. It is possible to assign a function to a variable or pass it to another function as a parameter. This may sound like a small feature, but it leads to an enormous number of possibilities, and allows software engineers to write software using functional programming techniques. These techniques will be discussed in detail in later chapters.

- Although JavaScript supports classes, its implementation of classes is somewhat confusing. This book will recommend that you avoid classes as far as possible and utilize prototyping techniques to create objects.

This book is not a tutorial on all features of the JavaScript language. Instead, this book will outline a set of fundamental approaches that software engineers can adopt with JavaScript.

If you have never taken the time to learn JavaScript before, and especially if you have only used statically typed languages, you will likely be impressed with the elegance and flexibility JavaScript syntax lends to its users.

JQuery

jQuery is a JavaScript library designed to simplify the process of writing JavaScript applications within web browsers.

Due to the document-centric nature of web pages, JavaScript is routinely responsible for selecting elements within the document (the internal representation of a document inside the browser is referred to as the Document Object Model), manipulating these elements, or reacting to events triggered by these elements. JavaScript natively supports this functionality through the Document Object Model API, which is also included in the HTML5 specification. jQuery essentially provides an elegant wrapper around the Document Object Model API.

The heart of jQuery is a selector engine. jQuery accepts selection criteria based on CSS style selectors, and returns a set of elements from the document that meet these criteria. Once a set of elements has been selected, jQuery provides a wide array of functions to perform operations on these elements, or to attach event listeners to them.

Although jQuery cannot do anything JavaScript could not do with the native DOM API, it has become enormously popular for several reasons:

- It removes the pain of dealing with quirks between different browsers.

- It provides a rich and succinct syntax that is seen by most as a vast improvement over the Document Object Model API.

- It is simple to write custom plugins for jQuery, and therefore it can be extended to meet specific needs.

- There are a wide range of open source plugins available for jQuery, including a popular UI toolkit called jQuery UI.

There are a number of competitors to jQuery such as Dojo and Prototype, but jQuery has obtained a critical mass in the market place and is almost a de-facto standard for web applications.

Cascading Style Sheets

Cascading Style Sheets provides a style sheet language for HTML. The majority of presentational features that remained in HTML from the pre-CSS days have now been removed in HTML5, and all presentation should now be performed entirely with CSS.

CSS provides a separation of concerns, and allows the styling of a page to change independently of its content, and vice versa. HTML is responsible for conveying the meaning of the web page, while CSS conveys its presentation.

This also means that the same content can be repurposed for different devices (such as mobile phones) by simply providing a new style sheet.

CSS provides a set of properties that describe how elements in a document should be styled when then match certain rules, and how these styles should interact with one another. The styles that can be applied to elements is mind-boggling, and has been significantly extended in CSS3, which is a specification largely running in parallel with HTML5.

It is usually not important for a software engineer to have an intimate knowledge of all CSS features, however it is important to understand the fundamentals, otherwise a huge amount of frustration and agony can ensue. As with all the languages addressed in this book, CSS is not as simple as it may appear, and a strong grasp of its fundamentals is important for anyone involved in the development of web applications.

I will largely ignore CSS during the development of the sample web application in this book. Appendix A provides an in-depth introduction to CSS, and you can skip to that chapter as required.

4 HTML5 MARKUP LANGUAGE

In this chapter we are going to look at the changes to the HTML markup language that have been included in the HTML5 specifications. The sample web application will use many, but by no means all of the new HTML5 tags, and a number of the attributes that have been added.

As mentioned above, the term HTML5 refers to both a markup language (a new version of HTML), and a set of APIs. HTML5 APIs will be covered in later chapters of this book.

Page structure

It is often good to start with the simplest possible example, for HTML5 that would be:

```
<!DOCTYPE html>

hello world!!!
```

Open your favorite text editor, enter the code above, save it as "hello.html" and open it in your favorite HTML5 compliant browser.

This may not look like an HTML page. For instance, there is no html tag and no body tag. Despite this, the browser knows what to do with the minimal content provided. If we analyze the Document Object Model generated for this page in the Chrome browser (open the Chrome Developer Tools and click the "Elements" tab) we will see the following:

```
<!DOCTYPE html>
▼ <html>
    <head></head>
    <body>hello world!!!
    </body>
  </html>
```

The browser has derived the intent of the HTML page and generated a compliant internal Document Object Model.

The HTML5 specification is very relaxed compared to earlier iterations of the specifications. Over the years there has been a move to stricter definitions of HTML, most noticeably HTML 4.01 Strict (published in 2000), and XHTML. These standards emphasized strict markup rules, such as always closing tags, and always placing quotes around attribute values. This drive for strictness was driven by a number of reasons:

- Earlier versions of HTML and XHTML were based on other markup languages (SGML and XML respectively), and this imposed restrictions on HTML.

- It is easier for browsers to derive the intent from documents written with strict rules, and this would help compatibility across browsers.

- It is easier for other tools to process documents if they comply with strict rules.

Despite the increasing strictness of the HTML and XHTML specifications, browsers never really enforced these rules. Browser vendors had long ago come to the realization that it was in their best interests to make the best of any markup they were given, regardless of its validity against relevant standards. From a browser vendor point of view the rationale is obvious: users will lose patience with a browser that refuses to render pages due to technicalities, and choose a browser that will.

A large discord had developed between browser vendors on the one hand, and the teams developing technical specifications on the other. This made no sense, since the technical specifications only had value if they were adopted by browser vendors. HTML5 has radically reversed this situation with a heavy dose of pragmatism.

As mentioned above, a large part of the HTML5 specification details how browsers should handle markup that would previously have been considered invalid. This is why Chrome could generate a Document Object Model from the "hello world" example. It is also why Firefox would generate exactly the same Document Object Model.

Despite the fact that the example above works, the following is probably the most appropriate skeleton to use when developing HTML5 compliant documents:

```
<!DOCTYPE html>

<html lang="en">

    <head>

        <meta charset="utf-8">

    </head>

    <body>

    </body>

</html>
```

I will explain the meaning of each section below, but before that we will add some content to the tasks.html document to make a start with the sample web application.

Throughout this book we are going to develop a task list application. The task list will include the following functionality:

- Users can create new tasks: this includes due dates and task categories.

24

- Users can edit tasks.

- Users can delete tasks.

- Users can view their task list.

- Overdue tasks are highlighted to users.

- Users can set tasks to complete.

Although this may seem a relatively simple web application, it contains enough complexity to show the important features of each language, but not so much complexity that the book becomes repetitive or focused on requirements.

We will begin by writing the markup that will form the basis of the task list screen. In this chapter all content will be static: in later chapters we will make this dynamic through the use of JavaScript and jQuery.

To begin the sample project, create a new folder anywhere on your file-system and add a file to it called tasks.html. This should contain the following content:

 Remember these examples can be downloaded from the book's website at cisdal.com/publishing.html. Each chapter has a zip file with all the examples.

```
<!DOCTYPE html>
<html lang="en">
<head>
<meta charset="utf-8">
<title>Task list</title>
<link rel="stylesheet" type="text/css" href="styles/tasks.css"
media="screen" />
</head>
<body>
  <header>
        <span>Task list</span>
    </header>
    <main>
        <section>
            <form>
                <div>
                    <label>Task</label> <input type="text"
required="required"
```

```
                    name="task" class="large"
placeholder="Breakfast at Tiffanys" />
                </div>
                <div>
                    <label>Required by</label> <input type="date"
required="required"
                        name="requiredBy" />
                </div>
                <div>
                    <label>Category</label> <select name="category">
                        <option value="Personal">Personal</option>
                        <option value="Work">Work
</option>
                    </select>
                </div>
                <nav>
                    <a href="#">Save task</a> <a href="#">Clear
task</a>
                </nav>
            </form>
        </section>
        <section>
            <table id="tblTasks">
                <colgroup>
                    <col width="50%">
                    <col width="25%">
                    <col width="25%">
                </colgroup>
                <thead>
                    <tr>
                        <th>Name</th>
                        <th>Due</th>
                        <th>Category</th>
                    </tr>
                </thead>
```

```
            <tbody>
                <tr>
                    <td>Return library books</td>
                    <td><time datetime="2013-10-14">2013-10-
14</time></td>
                    <td>Personal</td>
                </tr>
                <tr class="even">
                    <td>Perform project demo to stakeholders</td>
                    <td><time datetime="2013-10-14">2013-10-
14</time></td>
                    <td>Work</td>
                </tr>
                <tr>
                    <td>Meet friends for dinner</td>
                    <td><time datetime="2013-10-14">2013-10-
14</time></td>
                    <td>Personal</td>
                </tr>
            </tbody>
        </table>
        <nav>
            <a href="#">Add task</a>
        </nav>
    </section>
  </main>
  <footer>You have 3 tasks</footer>
</body>
</html>
```

As mentioned in the **head** section, this file has an accompanying CSS file. This should be placed in a sub-folder called "styles", and called "tasks.css":

```
@CHARSET "UTF-8";

body, h1, h2, h3, h4, h5, h6, p, ul, dl, ol, form, fieldset, input,
label, table, tbody, tfoot, th, tr, td, textarea, select {
  font-family: "helvetica neue", helvetica, "lucinda sans unicode",
"sans serif";
```

```
    font-weight: normal;
    color: #333;
    padding: 0;
    border: 0;
    margin: 0;
    font-size: 12px;
}

header {
    width:100%;
    height:80px;
    background:#d1e0e1;
    color: #333;
    font-weight: bold;
    font-size: 20px;
    text-align:center;
    line-height: 80px;
}

footer {
    width:100%;
    height:60px;
    background:#d1e0e1;
    font-size: 12px;
    text-align:center;
    line-height: 80px;
    margin-top:30px;
}

table, th, td
{
border: 1px solid #888;
}
```

```css
section {
    margin:20px 0 0 20px;
}


table {
    width:90%;
    border-collapse:collapse;
}


thead {
    line-height: 30px;
}


thead th {
    background: #53777a;
    color: #fff;
    font-size: 12px;
    font-weight: bold;
    text-align:center;
}


td {
    font-size: 11px;
    line-height: 25px;
    padding-left: 10px;
}


.even {
    background-color: #f8f8f8;
}


nav {
    margin:15px 0 10px 0;
}
```

```
nav a {
    background: #53777a;
    color: #fff;
    width: 80px;
    text-decoration: none;
    border: 1px solid #5b5b5b;
    font-size: 13px;
    text-align:  center;
    padding:5px 10px;
}

label {
    display: block;
    padding: 8px 0 8px 0;
    color: #333;
}

input {
    border-radius: 3px;
    height: 24px;
    border: 1px solid #AAA;
    padding: 0 7px;
}

input.large {
    width: 400px;
}

select {
    border: 1px solid #AAA;
    overflow: hidden;
    margin-right: 15px;
    width: 200px;
```

```
}


.required {
    color: red;
}


.not {
    display:none;
}


.rowIlighlight {
    font-weight:bold;
}


label.error {
    color: red;
            font-weight:bold;
}


.overdue {
    background: #F7DCE5;
}


.warning {
    background: #F7F7DC;
}


.taskCompleted {
    text-decoration: line-through;
}
```

When opened in a web browser, the HTML document will look as follows:

Task list

Task

Breakfast at Tiffanys

Required by

dd/mm/yyyy

Category

Personal

Save task   Clear task

Name	Due	Category
Return library books	2013-10-14	Personal
Perform project demo to stakeholders	2013-10-14	Work
Meet friends for dinner	2013-10-14	Personal

Add task

You have 3 tasks

There are a number of features that we should stop to discuss here.

Firstly, at the very top of the webpage, the DOCTYPE is simply:

```
<!DOCTYPE html>
```

 The DOCTYPE is an important signal to browsers and allows them to interpret the content of the document in the context of the rules associated with the document type. If this is omitted the browser will revert to its traditional rule set, and this may produce very different results.

You will also notice that there is no version number attached to html in the DOCTYPE. HTML should now be considered a living standard rather than a versioned standard with official releases, and this is reflected in the DOCTYPE. For this reason many people object to the term HTML5 entirely: it is just HTML.

The other thing you may notice about the DOCTYPE declaration is that it does not contain a reference to a Document Type Definition (DTD) document defining the rules of the markup language. This is a pleasant change for developers who may be accustomed to copy and pasting DOCTYPE declarations such as:

```
<!DOCTYPE HTML PUBLIC "-//W3C//DTD HTML 4.01//EN"
"http://www.w3.org/TR/html4/strict.dtd">
```

or

```
<!DOCTYPE html PUBLIC "-//W3C//DTD XHTML 1.1//EN"
"http://www.w3.org/TR/xhtml11/DTD/xhtml11.dtd">
```

The reason for this has already been touched upon: HTML5 is not based on SGML like earlier versions of HTML: in fact it is not based on anything.

Standard Generalized Markup Language (SGML) is a technology for defining the rules of markup languages such as XML or HTML.

Although HTML5 is not based on any other standards, it is possible to write HTML5 in XML serialization mode. The following would be the skeleton for an HTML5 page that serializes to XML (this is the equivalent of XHTML):

```html
<!DOCTYPE html>
<html xmlns="http://www.w3.org/1999/xhtml">
  <head>
    <meta charset="utf-8" />
  </head>
  <body>

  </body>
</html>
```

In addition, HTML5 documents that utilize "XML mode" should have a document type of application/xhtml+xml (rather than text/html).

We will not utilize XML mode in this book. In reality there are no real advantages to using an XML compliant version of HTML unless you need to process pages with an XML parser, but it is useful to know that this mode exists.

On the next line in the example above you will also notice that the html tag (which is optional) contains the language:

```html
<html lang="en">
```

The specification does not dictate what the language attribute will be used for, but obviously browsers can use the language for a variety of reasons, including offering translations to other languages.

Other than this, the only other feature you should add to every page is the following line in the head section to specify the character encoding:

```html
<meta charset="utf-8">
```

Unless you have a good reason, it is advisable to choose UTF-8 as the encoding. It is also important that you add this otherwise you may open your web application to a cross site scripting attack using UTF-7.

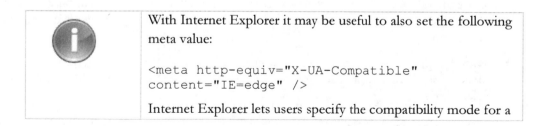 With Internet Explorer it may be useful to also set the following meta value:

```html
<meta http-equiv="X-UA-Compatible"
content="IE=edge" />
```

Internet Explorer lets users specify the compatibility mode for a

> document (since it supports backwards compatibility). This will guarantee that IE will use the latest mode for HTML5.

Tags

Since the advent of CSS, web designers have been relying on the **div** and **span** tags to layout content. These tags have no visual meaning; rather they act as containers for other elements. These containers can then be positioned anywhere on the screen using CSS.

The only difference between a **span** and a **div** is that **span**s are inline elements (they can be placed vertically adjacent to other elements) whereas **div**s are block elements, and therefore are positioned on their own line in the document.

 If this does not make sense, you may want to jump to Appendix A to understand CSS a little better.

Although **div** and **span** elements are sufficient for laying out complex websites (with the help of CSS), they lack semantic meaning. For instance, documents naturally contain headers and footers, but historically these have had to be represented with **div** elements.

The lack of semantic meaning inherent in **div** and **span** elements has been the subject of much criticism in the past. There is an argument that if a browser realizes that a section is a header or a footer it may choose to modify the way the document is presented, or repurpose the content, particularly on non-traditional devices such as mobile phones. As more and more devices support HTML based browsers, the need to repurpose content is likely to grow.

In addition, the lack of semantic meaning of **div** and **span** tags can make it difficult for a software engineer to modify an existing document. Not only can it be difficult to match up heavily nested **div** tags (and therefore it is easy to miss one), it may not be obvious what the purpose of each section in the document is.

HTML5 therefore provides an assortment of new tags that add semantic meaning to HTML documents. It is not intended that the browser will necessarily provide any visual implementation of these tags; for instance there is nothing to stop a **header** appearing at the bottom of the page and a **footer** appearing at the top of the page. In reality these tags are the visual equivalents of **div** and **span** tags – either inline or block containers with no other visual properties.

The following are the primary new semantic tags that have been added (ordered roughly according to usefulness):

- **section**: represents a generic document or section in an application. Using section correctly is part art, part science. A section should be self-contained, and capable of existing independently of other sections in the document. Examples can be seen in tasks.html.

- **header**: represents the introductory section of an HTML document or section of a document: there can be more than one header in a document. Examples can be seen in tasks.html.

- **footer**: represents information that should appear at the bottom of an HTML document or section. Again, there can be more than one footer in the document. Examples can be seen in tasks.html.

- **aside**: this is used for content that is loosely associated with other content around it, but which could be considered separate. An aside will often be visually separated from the content around it with a border or font.

- **article**: this should be used to separate content that can be distributed independently from other content in the document. An example may be a blog post, or a review. This is similar to section, but article should only be used for separating content, not generic sections of the document.

- **details**: contains additional details that a user can choose to show or hide by clicking the summary tag.

- **summary**: contains a summary of the contents that appear in the details tag. The idea behind this is that the summary can be shown to the user when the document loads, and they can select to view the details if they wish to. The details/summary tags are therefore intended to be implemented as interactive tags (clicking them causes an action to occur), but currently this is only supported by Chrome.

- **main**: this should be used to surround the main section of a document, stripped of all headers, footers, asides and menus. Unlike other tags, this should only be used once per page. This tag should surround the content that forms the central functionality or content of the document. Examples can be seen in tasks.html.

- **nav**: contains a set of navigation links such as those that commonly appear in the header section of a web page.

- **dialog**: used for dialog boxes and windows. This element supports an attribute called open that indicates if the dialog is active to the user.

- **wbr**: this is used as a hint to the browser that it could add a line break. This can be useful if a browser is adding line breaks in the wrong place due to a long word.

- **mark**: this can be used to indicate that a piece of text is highlighted. Browsers will add a background color to the text, which can be configured with CSS.

- **figure**: this element can be used to surround self-contained content such as photos and illustrations. This element uses the block display type rather than the inline-block display type (as used for images)

- **figcaption**: this is used for providing a legend for a figure.

- **address**: defines a section describing contact information.

It is important not to overuse these new tags. The new tags have specific meaning, and if you need to separate content for other purposes, including stylistic purposes (via CSS), there is nothing wrong with using **div** and **span** tags.

In addition, don't expect these tags to radically change your life. In reality they are one of the least interesting features of HTML5. Even the often quoted benefit of these tags, "repurposing", is probably more hype that reality.

As an example of repurposing, consider Safari's "Reader" mode. This cuts out all the superfluous content from a page containing an article, and therefore makes the article easier to read. It may have been easier for Apple to implement this if everyone used the article tag: but Apple still managed to implement this feature without it. In addition, it is unlikely Apple would simply trust the semantic tags presented by a page, since websites would quickly learn the benefits of placing advertising material inside an article element, even though the specification implies they should be outside it.

There are a number of other new tags that are directly related to functional aspects of pages (such as video and audio): these will be addressed separately.

Microformats

If you look at the **time** tags in the document you will see the following:

```
<time datetime="2013-10-14">2013-10-14</time>
```

This could also have been written:

```
<time datetime="2013-10-14">14th October</time>
```

Or

```
<time datetime="2013-10-14">October 2014</time>
```

The important aspect of this tag is that it contains the same information twice. The first version of the date is presented in an attribute, and conforms to the ISO standards for dates (and times if required). The second version appears between the tags, and is the version that will be displayed to the user.

The purpose of this feature is to provide a machine and human readable version of the same information. Features such as this are referred to as "microformats", and are widely used on the Internet to provide semantic meaning to search engines and other automated clients, while providing human friendly versions of the same data to humans.

Microformats have not been officially included in the HTML5 specification, although the time tag is an example of a microformat. There are several standards for additional microformats, and it is likely that HTML5 will be expanded in time to support these.

HTML5 Forms

There are a number of additions in HTML5 to forms, and the input fields they contain. Form elements such as input fields and select boxes had not really changed since the early versions of HTML. Not only does HTML5 introduce a new set of input types, it includes a large set of attributes for customising form inputs, along with native validation of form fields.

New Input Types

If you look at the input type of the field named "requiredBy" you will notice that its type is set to date:

```
<input type="date" required="required"name="requiredBy"/>
```

> It is also valid, and possibly preferable, to write this as
>
> ```
> <input type="date" required
> name="requiredBy"/>
> ```
>
> HTML5 does not require all attributes to have values. These attributes are referred to as Boolean attributes, since their presence indicates true, and their absence indicates false.
>
> It is arguably preferable to omit the value because it avoids the possibility of believing the following is valid:
>
> ```
> required="false"
> ```

It is the expectation of the HTML5 specification that the browser will provide the user some way to choose a date when they click on such a field, although the exact mechanism is left up to browser vendors.

Some browsers do not currently support the **date** input type, and in those cases it acts just like a **text** input type.

When browsers choose to implement one of the new input types they can decide on the best way to implement it based on the specifics of the device they are running on. For instance, the date input type on the iPad displays the following calendar:

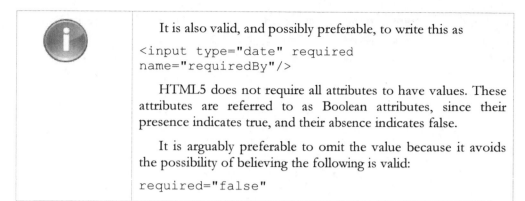

This looks very different to the date input type presented by Chrome on a desktop:

In addition to the date input type, HTML5 has several other new input types. Many of these such as:

- email
- url
- tel (telephone)
- number

offer the most advantage to devices that use software based keyboards. In these cases the device can present the user with a set of keys best suited to the input type. For instance, if the type was **email** the keyboard may present the user with the alphabetic characters, the "@" symbol, the "." and maybe a special ".com" key.

Mobile devices in particular offer interesting possibilities for input types such as **tel** and **email**, since the browser could potentially autocomplete these based on details in the mobile phone's phonebook.

HTML5 validation (which will be introduced below) can also validate that these fields contain valid values for their specified type.

In addition, HTML5 offers the following input types which, like the date input type, are expected to present the user with a widget to simplify the choice of a value:

- color
- datedatetime
- datetime-local
- month

- range

- search

- time

- week

In reality most of these types cannot be relied on in most browsers. This is a familiar problem for developers of web applications, so it is worth stopping to discuss the concept of "polyfills", which are a common solution to this problem.

A polyfill is an elegant solution to the problem that some features are supported by a subset of browsers. If a feature is natively supported in a particular browser, the polyfill does nothing. If the feature is not supported, the polyfill provides an implementation, usually via a JavaScript library.

In order to utilize polyfills, the following two features are required:

1. The ability to detect whether a browser supports a particular feature.

2. The ability to provide an implementation for this feature dynamically using JavaScript. Even where it is possible to detect a feature is missing, it may not be possible to provide an implementation.

Although it is often trivial to provide both of these features in your own code, it is always preferable to use well tested existing libraries where possible. The most popular library for detecting supported features is Modernizr, and can be found at http://modernizr.com/.

With Modernizr in place, feature detection is as simple as this:

```
if (Modernizr.canvas) {
    // do nothing
} else {
    // provide implementation
}
```

In addition to feature detection, Modernizr also contains a large list of polyfill implementations that can be utilized, or you can write your own.

HTML5 also offers native support for two entirely new form elements:

- **Progress**: this provides a native implementation of a progress bar that can be updated through changes to the progress bar attributes.

- **Meter**: this provides a scalar measurement within a defined range. It allows a number to be selected within a range by dragging a knob along a slider.

These new elements will prove enormously useful when fully implemented in all browsers, until then however it is likely you will need to rely on alternatives offered by libraries such as jQuery UI.

New Attributes on Input types

In addition to the new input types, a large number of new attributes are supported on input types.

Attributes are used to control how an element works.

Many of these attributes are provided to support native HTML validation, these include:

- **required**: this indicates that a value is mandatory for the field in order to submit the form.

- **maxlength**: this is used on text based input fields to specify the maximum length of the input.

- **min** and **max**: these are used on number, date and range based input fields to specify minimum and maximum values.

- **pattern**: these are used whenever input must conform to a regular expression pattern. Most browsers provide default implementations for types such as email.

- **formnovalidate**: This can be applied to a submit button in order to disable validation. In addition, the **novalidate** attribute can be applied to the form to achieve the same result.

The validation of form elements will be introduced in later chapters.

A number of other attributes have been added to provide commonly requested functionality:

- **placeholder**: This provides a greyed out placeholder in an input field. This can be used to provide context to a user, and act as a hint to the purpose of a field.

- **autocomplete**: When autocomplete is added, the browser will suggest values to the user as they type.

- **autofocus**: This can be used to automatically give a particular field focus when the document loads. Previously this could only be achieved through JavaScript.

- **form**: it is possible to denote an input field as part of a form even when it is not nested inside the form. This also allows an input field to be included in multiple forms.

- **formaction**: It is possible to provide a **formaction** attribute on a submit button to override the action set on the form itself. This is particularly useful when there are multiple submit buttons in the same form. The attribute **formenctype** can be used in conjunction with this to override the content type (**enctype**) set on the form itself, and **formmethod** can be used to override the form's default method (e.g. POST).

- **step**: This can be used on number, date or range input fields. The intention is that the input field will provide up and down arrows, and pressing this will increment or decrement the current value by the step amount.

Other new features

The HTML5 markup language contains many other new features that are outside the scope of this book. This section will provide a very brief introduction to these features so you know they exist, without going into detail about how they work.

HTML5 provides a **canvas** element that allows for 2D drawing and animation. This is one of the features of HTML5 that is intended to provide an alternative to Adobe Flash. There are many interesting demos available on the Internet showing the power of this feature.

The canvas element covers some of the same scope as **Scalable Vector Graphics** (SVG), which is not technically part of HTML5, but is still a relatively new, and useful feature of web browsers.

WebGL provides similar capabilities to Canvas, but allows for 3D rendering. The main draw back for WebGL is that not as many browsers support it as the Canvas, which has universal support amongst the main browser vendors. Where it is supported, the support is often partial.

Another feature of HTML5 that drew a lot of attention are the **audio** and **video** tags. Currently Adobe Flash is the de-facto standard for video in particular, largely because of its ubiquity and the fact YouTube used it. The **audio** and **video** elements are intended to allow web site developers to embed audio and video in web sites without the need for plugins.

Ever since the early days of web site development back buttons have caused issues. This has become even more apparent with modern web applications that often do not rely on page refreshes, even when users think they have changed pages. By default, this means the back button tends not to do what users expect in a large number of scenarios. The **Session History Management** API allows the developer finer-grained control over the history of a tab, and therefore allows for more intuitive behaviour from the Back and Forward buttons.

5 JAVASCRIPT FUNDAMENTALS

This section will provide an in-depth overview of JavaScript, including its strengths and weaknesses. The intention of this chapter is to provide you a strong understanding of JavaScript fundamentals, and to focus on how the language *should* be used, rather than how it *can* be used.

JavaScript is a particularly flexible language, and does not enforce much discipline or structure on its users. In addition, JavaScript contains a number of features than can only truly be regarded as bugs. These remain in the language principally due to backwards compatibility concerns.

In order to write large-scale web applications it is necessary to harness the strengths of JavaScript, while at the same time avoiding the pitfalls that can easily confront software engineers and programmers who do not understand the language fundamentals, and do not structure their applications in a manner compatible with the growth of the code base.

As mentioned in the introduction, this chapter will not act as a tutorial on the syntax of JavaScript (such as loops and branching), although anyone familiar with languages utilizing similar syntax (C, C++, Java etc.), will quickly pick up those details from the examples below.

In order to follow the examples in this book, simply open the Chrome or Firefox console, and enter the commands directly (as demonstrated earlier in the book).

Types

Any understanding of JavaScript begins with an understanding of its data types, and how these types are used.

JavaScript has the following data types:

- String
- Number
- Boolean
- Null
- Undefined

- Object

Each of these will be outlined in the sections below.

Strings

Strings are series of characters enclosed in either single or double quotes:

```
> "hello world"
```

```
"hello world"
```

```
> 'hello world'
```

```
"hello world"
```

The examples above are referred to as string literals. We can also assign a string to a variable:

```
> s = 'Hello world'
```

```
"Hello world"
```

 When using the console, variables will not be declared with the **var** keyword. As you will see below, it is critical that this is used in most situations when writing actual JavaScript code.

We can then inspect the type of this variable using the **typeof** operator:

```
> typeof s
```

```
"string"
```

Although strings are their own data type, it is possible to invoke methods on them just as we will see it is possible to invoke methods on objects below.

```
> s.charAt(1)
```

```
"e"
```

```
> s.substr(6)
```

```
"world"
```

```
> s.toUpperCase()
```

```
"HELLO WORLD"
```

In addition, strings have properties that can be accessed, just as we will see on objects in the examples below:

```
> s.length
```

```
11
```

JavaScript strings are largely equivalent to strings in Java. One consequence of this is that strings are immutable.

 An immutable object is an object that cannot be changed after it is first created. Even when these appear to change, as in the examples below, in reality a new object is being created.

In order to see immutability in action, declare a new variable called **t**, and assign it the value of **s**:

```
> t = s
```

```
"Hello world"
```

We can now print out the value of **t**, and also confirm that **t** and **s** are equal:

```
> t
```

```
"Hello world"
```

```
> s == t
```

```
true
```

What should happen if we now modify the string held against the variable **s**? We can append to the string value using the **+=** operator:

```
> s += 'test'
```

```
"Hello worldtest"
```

If you now print out the value of **s** you will see that the string's value appears to have changed:

```
> s
```

```
"Hello worldtest"
```

Despite this, if you print out the value of **t** it has retained its old value:

```
> t
```

```
"Hello world"
```

When we appended "test" to the string held against the variable **s**, the underlying string was not modified; instead a new string was created and assigned to the variable **s**. Since **t** still refers to the original string, it is not impacted by the modification.

Numbers

The number type is used to represent both integer and floating-point values; in fact all numbers are 64 bit floating-point numbers in JavaScript:

```
> n = 6.827
```

```
6.827
```

```
> typeof n
```

```
"number"
```

```
> n2 = 6
```

```
6
```

```
> typeof n2
```

```
"number"
```

Due to the fact that all numbers are floating-point, operations between two integers can return floating-point results (unlike in Java).

```
> 1/3
```

```
0.3333333333333333
```

In addition to real numbers, JavaScript also supports a number of special values.

"Not a number" is used in cases where an arithmetic operation produces a result that is not a number. Confusingly, the type of this value is still a **number**.

```
> a = 9/undefined
```

```
NaN
```

```
> typeof a
```

```
"number"
```

It would have potentially been more useful for JavaScript to generate an error in this scenario.

Negative and positive infinity are also supported, and are most often generated when dividing by 0:

```
> b = 6/0
```

```
Infinity
```

```
> b == Number.POSITIVE_INFINITY
```

```
true
```

```
> c = -6/0
```

```
-Infinity
```

```
> c == Number.NEGATIVE_INFINITY
```

```
true
```

Again, most programming languages would generate errors where an integer is divided by 0. Since all numbers are floating point in JavaScript, however, it follows the IEEE standard of using infinity. The rationale for this is that the divisor may not be 0: it may be a very small number that can only be represented as 0 due to the limitations of the bits available for storing the number.

JavaScript also natively supports a Math library modeled almost identically on the Java equivalent. Most common math functions are available in this library.

```
> Math.pow(3, 2)
```

```
9
```

```
> Math.round(3.22)
```

```
3
```

Booleans

JavaScript supports a boolean type that contains the literal values **true** and **false**:

```
> t = true
```

```
true
```

```
> typeof t
```

```
"boolean"
```

```
> f = false
```

```
false
```

Equality operators in JavaScript (>, <, ==, !=, >=, <=) also return booleans as their result:

```
> f != t
```

```
true
```

Null

Null is a data type that has a single value: **null**.

```
> n   = null
```

```
null
```

Confusingly, **null** is considered to be of type object:

```
> typeof n
```

```
"object"
```

This is another bug in the JavaScript language that has been maintained for backwards compatibility. Despite this, **null** is genuinely a unique data type in JavaScript.

It is possible to set a variable to **null** after it has been assigned a value, therefore removing the reference to its current value (and changing its data type):

```
> q = 2

2

> typeof q

"number"

> q = null

null

> typeof q

"object"
```

Undefined

The **undefined** data type is returned when you access a property on an object that does not exist, or use a variable before it is declared, or before it is assigned a value.

```
> typeof g

"undefined"
```

Objects

Other than the types outlined above, all data types in JavaScript are objects: this includes arrays, functions, dates and user defined objects. Objects will be discussed at length in the sections below.

Truthy and Falsey Values

Now that you have an understanding of the JavaScript data types, the next thing to understand is that some values for these types evaluate to **true**, and some evaluate to **false**. For instance, the following are all considered false in JavaScript:

- false

- 0 (zero)
- "" (empty string)
- null
- undefined
- NaN

In order to see this in action, simply ask if they are equal to **false** in the console:

```
> 0 == false
```

```
true
```

All other values represent **true** values.

As a consequence of this, it is possible to utilize a shortcut when evaluating the value of variables in conditional statements. Instead of writing the following:

```
> if (a == undefined || a == null) {
    a = 1;
}
```

It is possible to simply write:

```
> if (!a) {
    a = 10
}
```

Likewise, if you only want to use a variable if it has a value you can write the following:

```
> if (s) {
    console.log(s)
}
```

This shortcut is enormously useful, and extensively used in JavaScript code.

The final thing that should be understood is which values are equal to one another; the following may come as a surprise:

```
> null == undefined
```

```
true
```

```
> 5 == "5"
```

```
true
```

```
> "true" == true
```

```
false
```

```
> "1" == true
```

```
true
```

```
> "2" == true
```

```
false
```

There are numerous inconsistencies in the examples above, and again, these are often bugs rather than features. **Null** should not be considered equal to **undefined**, despite the fact they are both falsey values they represent very different data-types and meanings.

Fortunately, JavaScript contains an alternative pair of equality operators:

```
===
```

```
!==
```

These compare variables based on both their value and their data type, and therefore provide more expected results:

```
> null === undefined
```

```
false
```

```
> 5 === "5"
```

```
false
```

```
> "true" === true
```

```
false
```

```
> "1" === true
```

```
false
```

It is best practice to always use these equality operators unless you consciously want to compare two values you know have different data types.

 If you want to know whether any value is true or false in a Boolean sense, you can print it out by prepending !! to it. A single ! will negate a Boolean value, while !! provides a double negative, and therefore prints out the Boolean value of any value:

```
!!""
```

```
false
```

```
!!"hello"
```

```
true
```

Dynamic Typing

Finally, it is worth reiterating that JavaScript is a dynamically typed language.

Languages such as Java and C++ are statically typed languages. In statically typed languages, all variables are assigned a type at compile time, and this type cannot be changed.

 The terms strong and weak typing are sometimes used to refer to statically typed and dynamically typed languages respectively.

In a statically typed language, the compiler can perform type checking: if a variable is defined to store an integer, the compiler can check that it is not assigned a string. This catches many causes of bugs before they can become an issue at run-time.

As we have seen, JavaScript variables derive their types based on the values they are assigned at run-time, and variables can change their type if they are assigned a new value. As a result it is not possible to perform static type checking in JavaScript, e.g. to ensure a string is not provided where a number is expected.

Consider the following function that adds two numbers together:

```
function add(v1, v2) {
    return v1+v2;
}
```

If you invoke this function with two numbers, the result is as expected:

```
> add(1,1)
```

```
2
```

If you accidentally pass a string as one of the parameters however, the result is very different:

```
> add(1,"1")
```

```
"11"
```

Instead of adding the numbers, JavaScript has performed string concatenation between the number and the string. It is unlikely that this is the result expected. This is one reason why the **typeof** operator is so important in JavaScript, it allows the function above to be rewritten as follows:

```
function add(v1, v2) {
  if (typeof v1 === "number"
          && typeof v2 === "number") {
      return v1+v2;
  } else {
    throw "both arguments must be numbers";
  }
}
```

This at least ensures data type issues will be identified at run-time, even if it does not highlight these issues to the programmer who wrote the code allowing the function to be called incorrectly.

> Using the "+" operator on different data types produces a variety of random results in JavaScript:
>
> ```
> {} + [] = 0
> [] + {} = Object
> ```
>
> Even using the "+" operator on the same data types can produce meaningless results:
>
> ```
> [] + [] = empty string
> {} + {} = NaN
> ```
>
> It is hard to make sense of any of these results.
>
> In addition, the "-" operator should only be used on numbers:
>
> ```
> "a" + 1 = "a1"
> "a" - 1 = NaN
> ```

There are many arguments for and against dynamically typed languages. This book will not address these arguments, but it is safe to conclude that dynamic typing has advantages, but those come at the risks of run-time bugs.

Objects

JavaScript also supports objects; in fact, most values in JavaScript applications will be objects. JavaScript also supports syntax for defining classes that objects can be instantiated from. This may lead you to think JavaScript is a conventional object orientated language – this would be a mistake.

In classical object orientated languages such as Java and C#, classes must be defined before objects can be instantiated from them. It is never possible to have an object that is not a type of a specific class.

Classes are static templates that contain definitions of the properties and methods that objects will contain. During program execution, instances of these classes are created: these are called objects. All objects instantiated from the same class have the same properties and methods, although the values assigned to properties will differ from instance to instance.

When designing applications with a classical object orientated language you may find cases where you would like some objects to contain additional properties or methods, even though they are similar in other respects to those created by an existing class. For instance you may have started with a class called "Vehicle" which contained the following properties:

1. Registration number

2. Initial year of registration

3. Make of vehicle

4. Model of vehicle

Objects can be instantiated from this class, and will contain four properties to which values can be assigned.

 This book will use the term "property" to refer to the state of an object. Other languages may call these fields or attributes.

You may subsequently decide that you would like to capture more information about trucks, for instance:

- Number of axles

- Towing capacity

You cannot simply add these new properties to objects that have been created from the Vehicle class; you must first create a new class (called Truck), and extend the Vehicle class. Only when the class structure is in place can you begin creating instances of Trucks.

A further feature of classes is that they must be defined when the application is compiled; they cannot be defined on the fly at run-time. It is not possible to decide midway through program execution that you would like to start capturing an additional property on some objects.

JavaScript has a far more flexible attitude to classes and objects, in fact classes are not essential to

JavaScript programming at all.

The simplest way you can create a new object in JavaScript is as follows:

```
> obj = {}
```

The **typeof** operator confirms that the **obj** variable is indeed an object:

```
> typeof obj
"object"
```

If you are familiar with classical object orientated languages you may wonder what *type* **obj** is? This object is not of any type; it is just an object.

It may sound difficult to write code without knowing the type. For instance, if a function is passed an object without knowing its type, how does it know what to do with it?

JavaScript uses an approach colloquially known as "duck typing". There is an old saying, "if it walks like a duck, and swims like a duck, and quacks like a duck, it probably is a duck". Likewise, in JavaScript we might say "If it has a registration number property, and has a year of registration property, it probably is a vehicle".

An empty object with no properties or methods is not very useful. With JavaScript however, it is possible to dynamically add properties and methods:

```
> obj.firstName = 'John';


> obj.lastName = 'Smith';


> obj.age = 32;


> obj.increaseAge = function() {
    this.age++;
}
```

 In order to type commands that span multiple lines, hold down the Shift key while pressing enter.

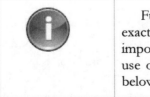 Functions inside objects are referred to as methods. They are exactly the same as functions, except in the way they treat an important variable called **this**. You may have also noticed the use of **this** in the method above: this will be explained in full below.

If you now look at the object in the JavaScript console you will see that it has a set of properties with values assigned:

```
> obj
```

```
Object {firstName: "John", lastName: "Smith", age: 32, increaseAge:
function}
```

The reason this is possible is because objects in JavaScript are really just associative arrays (also known as hash maps in other languages). Associative arrays are supported natively in most programming languages, and comprise a collection of name/value pairs.

In order to access a property on a JavaScript object, simply use the following notation:

```
> obj.firstName
```

```
"John"
```

JavaScript supports an alternative syntax for accessing and setting properties that is even more evocative of associative arrays in other languages.

```
> obj['firstName']
```

```
"John"
```

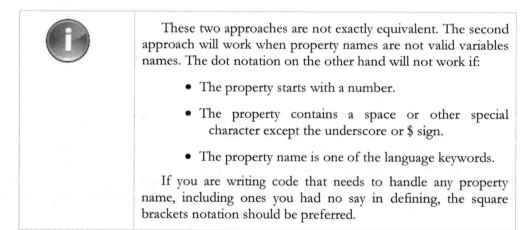

These two approaches are not exactly equivalent. The second approach will work when property names are not valid variables names. The dot notation on the other hand will not work if:

- The property starts with a number.
- The property contains a space or other special character except the underscore or $ sign.
- The property name is one of the language keywords.

If you are writing code that needs to handle any property name, including ones you had no say in defining, the square brackets notation should be preferred.

In addition to properties, the example above provides an example of a method being added to an object. The method **increaseAge** increments the age property by 1: it can be invoked as follows:

```
> obj.increaseAge()
```

```
> obj.age
```

33

I alluded to the use of the **this** variable inside the method:

```
obj.increaseAge = function() {

    this.age++;

}
```

This is the only thing that separates a function from a method: in a method the special variable **this** refers to the object itself, and therefore:

```
this.age
```

is a way of accessing the **age** property on the object. As we will see in future sections, **this** takes on several different meanings depending on context. Understanding the meaning of **this** in these different contexts is one of the keys to understanding JavaScript.

Although it is possible to construct objects without any reliance on classes, it is probably obvious that we are also missing out on the benefits that classes bring.

If you want to create a new object to refer to a different person, you need to add these properties and methods all over again. This is not a major problem for the properties of an object, since you would need to provide values for those properties anyway, but it is a major inconvenience for methods. For instance, you would need to write the following:

```
> obj2 = {}


> obj2.firstName = 'Albert'


> obj2.lastName = 'Jones'


> obj2.age = 28


> obj2.increaseAge = function() {

    this.age++;

}
```

> An alternative approach is to include the properties and methods inside the {} separating properties/methods with commas, and properties/methods from their values with colons:
>
> ```
> obj2 = {
>
>     firstName: 'Albert',
>
>     lastName: 'Jones',
>
>     age: 28,
> ```

```
                              increaseAge: function() {
                                   this.age++;
                              }
                         }
```

This is going to become a major inconvenience, especially if you have a large number of methods on your object.

There is a solution to this problem that does not rely on reverting to classes: you could simply clone an existing object, and change its properties as required. The object being cloned can be referred to as a prototype for other objects.

We will see in later chapters that jQuery contains a helper for cloning objects, but for now we will write our own clone implementation. This function will perform a deep clone on an object: if a property on an object contains a value that is an object, that object will also be cloned.

```
function clone(obj) {
    if (obj == null || typeof obj != 'object') {
        return obj;
    }
    var newObj = {}
    for (var key in obj) {
        newObj[key] = clone(obj[key]);
    }
    return newObj;
}
```

This function uses the **for (var key in obj)** loop to iterate through all the properties on an object. This is a special kind of JavaScript loop specifically provided to iterate through properties in an object. If the value of the property is an object, it is recursively passed to the **clone** function. If it is a simple type (such as a number or string) it is returned immediately so it can be set directly on the new instance of the object. You will remember from earlier sections that strings and numbers are immutable; therefore they do not need to be cloned.

This implementation should reinforce to you how simple JavaScript objects are.

> There are potential problems with this implementation that have been ignored for simplicity. This implementation should not be used in real applications: use versions provided in the jQuery or Underscore libraries.

You can now use this function to construct a new object for storing information about people:

```
> obj3 = clone(obj2)
```

```
> obj3.firstName = 'Jim'

"Jim"

> obj3.firstName = 'Duffey'

"Duffey"

> obj3.age = 42

> obj3.increaseAge()

43
```

As you can see we have retained the method already defined on its prototype.

This section is not intended to imply classes have no value in JavaScript, instead it is intended to demonstrate what objects truly are in JavaScript, and to suggest that there are viable ways of writing JavaScript that does not utilize classes.

There are potential pitfalls in this implementation. For instance, if you forget to set a property on the newly cloned object, it will retain the value from the object it was cloned from: this may or may not be correct, and could become a source of bugs.

Although we will examine more advanced approaches to object creation below, the approach to objects examined in this section has a lot to recommend it.

JavaScript Object Notation

The previous section demonstrated how simple JavaScript objects are. At heart, JavaScript objects are simple associative arrays. Each property in the object can have a value that is a simple type (such as a number or a string), a function, an array, or another type of object.

When writing web-based applications it is often necessary to send data from the client to the server, or the server to the client. In order to transfer data across a network it must be encoded in a data format agreed by both the sender and the receiver.

There are many data formats that can be used to send and receive data; of these XML is probably the most common. An example XML document for representing people might look as follows:

```
<person>
    <firstName>John</firstName>
    <lastName>Smith</lastName>
    <age>32</age>
```

```
<address>
    <city>Los Angeles</city>
    <postCode>90245</postCode>
</address>
</person>
```

XML is a widely used data format, particularly in enterprise applications. It has many benefits, including a wide array of libraries that support it and widespread acceptance in IT departments. XML is a particularly verbose data format however, in the example above far more than 75% of the text is made up of tags rather than content.

Before gaining an understanding of JSON, first consider what a JavaScript object may look like that contained this same data:

```
> person = {};
```

```
> person.firstName = 'John';
```

```
> person.lastName = 'Smith';
```

```
> person.age = 32;
```

```
> person.address = {};
```

```
> person.address.city = 'Los Angeles';
```

```
> person.address.postCode = 90245;
```

The example above consists of two objects. The first object is a person; this then contains a second object that captures the address information.

It would not be difficult to create an object from the XML structure. There is however a data format that is far more closely aligned with JavaScript called the JavaScript Object Notation (JSON) that makes this process trivial.

You can transform this object into a JSON encoded string as follows:

```
> JSON.stringify(person)
```

```
"{"firstName":"John","lastName":"Smith","age":32,"address":{"city":"Los Angeles","postCode":90245}}"
```

The output of this function call is a string, and could be assigned to a variable:

```
> s = JSON.stringify(person)
```

A string can then be transformed back into an object as follows:

```
> person2 = JSON.parse(s)
```

The process of converting between a string and an object is called serializing and de-serializing: the string is a serialized form of the object.

 This process is only applicable for properties: methods are not retained when an object is serialized.

JSON is a remarkably simple data format. The entire data format is contained in a couple of paragraphs at the following web site:

http://www.json.org/

There are 3 types of value in JSON:

1. **Objects**, denoted with the now familiar curly brackets

2. **Arrays**, which are denoted by [] brackets, and contain comma separated values just like JavaScript arrays.

3. **Literal values** (strings, numbers, Booleans)

An object or an array can in turn contain any of these 3 types. For instance, an array may contain an object, an object may contain an array, an object may contain another object, etc.

JavaScript makes it possible to convert from a *stringified* version to an *object* representation purely because the language does not rely on classes. The stringified version of the object does not contain information on what type it is: it is simply a set of properties formatted according to the JSON specification. Likewise though, JavaScript does not need to know what type of object needs to be created when de-serializing: it can simply add the appropriate properties to an otherwise empty object.

JSON has become a widely used data format even for applications that do not use JavaScript. For instance, Java contains libraries for converting to and from JSON. The only difference in languages such as Java is that you must tell the library what type of class the textual string represents.

 Java can in fact de-serialize a string into an object without knowing the type, but it needs to use hash maps rather than programmer defined classes.

One reason for the widespread adoption of JSON (beyond its simplicity) is the fact it is far less verbose than XML – the example above is roughly half the size of the XML version. Although the size is far smaller, it is still easy for a human to read and understand a JSON encoded message (which was a traditional strength XML had over other data formats, particularly binary data formats).

As we go through the book we will explore several cases where this ability to convert simply and easily from an object to a textual string is enormously useful.

Prototypes

We will return now to our discussion of objects in JavaScript.

The **clone** function that we wrote above was our first attempt at code reuse. It allowed us to reuse or extend an object that we had already written. One problem discussed with the **clone** function was that it took all the properties from the object it was cloning, including properties that were specific to the cloned instance, such as **firstName** and **lastName**.

JavaScript provides a more elegant mechanism for extending objects called prototypes. In fact, JavaScript itself is considered a prototype-based language.

If you declare an empty object, you may think that it contains no properties at all:

```
> obj = {}
```

You can however execute the following method on the object:

```
> obj.toString()
```

```
"[object Object]"
```

Where did the **toString** method come from?

All JavaScript objects have a prototype object (this can be **null** in rare instances, but this scenario can largely be ignored). A prototype object is an object in its own right, and can encapsulate properties and methods. If we access a property or method on an object, JavaScript will first try to access that property or method on the object itself. If the object has no property or method with that name it will look for it on the prototype object.

In fact, there can be a whole chain of objects due to the fact that the object that is our prototype may itself have a prototype. If no objects in the prototype chain have a property matching the name specified then JavaScript returns a special type called **undefined**.

The prototype of our empty object was provided by **Object.prototype**. This is the only object that does not have a prototype of its own, and therefore is the end of the chain.

In order to see the prototype chain in action, we can define our own **toString** implementation on the empty object.

```
> obj.toString = function() {
    return "I am an object"
};
```

If we now execute **toString** on this object, the newly defined version will be used:

```
> obj.toString()
```

```
"I am an object"
```

In this case you have not modified the implementation of **toString** on the prototype; it has been overridden on this specific instance. In order to prove this, you can create a new empty object, and execute the **toString** method on it:

```
>. obj2 = {}
```

```
> obj2.toString()
```

```
"[object Object]"
```

The properties on a prototype are immutable, just like strings are immutable. Although all objects with the same prototype share the properties on the prototype, they cannot change the prototype; they simply override these properties on themselves.

The specific prototype assigned to objects created with the object literal notation is the **Object.prototype**. Different objects can however have different prototypes. For instance, if we create an array using the array literal notation, the variable is still an object:

```
> a = [1,2,3,4,5];
```

```
> typeof a
```

```
"object"
```

Because this is an object, it will contain the Object prototype somewhere in its hierarchy, and therefore we can invoke the **toString** method. You will notice that the **toString** implementation has been specially tailored for arrays:

```
> a.toString()
```

```
"1,2,3,4,5"
```

The array instance also has access to a whole set of other properties that were not available to our object created with the object literal notation:

```
> a.reverse()
```

```
[5, 4, 3, 2, 1]
```

```
> a.pop()
```

```
1
```

```
> a.push(6)
```

```
5
```

These methods are derived from the prototype object for arrays called **Array.prototype** (which in turn has Object.prototype as its prototype).

Due to the fact that all arrays are based on the same prototype, if we add methods to this prototype, they immediately become available to all arrays. Remember, prototypes are just objects themselves; therefore they can be modified just like any other object.

For instance, arrays do not have a "contains" method. It might be useful to implement a method that accepts a single parameter, and then returns true if the array contains that value. This can be written as follows:

```
> Array.prototype.contains = function (val) {

    for (var i = 0; i < this.length; i++) {

        if (this[i] === val) {

            return true;

        }

    }

    return false;

}
```

We can now execute the following:

```
> [1,2,3,4,5].contains(3)
```

```
true
```

```
> a.contains(6)
```

```
false
```

Adding functionality to prototypes is a very effective code reuse pattern. As soon as the functionality is added to that prototype, it is immediately available to all objects that contain that prototype in their prototype chain: even if they were created before the functionality was added to the prototype.

 If you are wondering how objects can be given a specific prototype, this will be explained in more detail below.

Prototypes provide a mechanism to tidy up the code reuse pattern that we used earlier. The new implementation of **clone** (which we will rename to **extends**) still accepts an object, but now returns a new empty object with that object set as its prototype.

We will first write the object that will act as the prototype. This is going to contain two methods, the increase age method we saw earlier, and a new method that returns the full name of the person as the concatenation of the first and last name. In addition, this implementation is going to combine object creation, and the addition of methods to the object, into a single step:

```
> person = {
    getFullName: function() {
        return this.firstName+" "+this.lastName;
    },
    increaseAge: function() {
        this.age++;
    }
}
```

Notice that this object is referring to properties that are **undefined**. It does not include **lastName**, **firstName** or **age** properties, therefore calling these methods will not produce very useful results:

```
> person.getFullName()
```

```
"undefined undefined"
```

We will now write an **extends** function that accepts this object as a parameter, and returns a new object with this object set as its prototype:

```
function extend(obj) {
    function E(){};
    E.prototype = obj;
    return new E();
}
```

This code may look unfamiliar or mysterious. That is because this function is taking advantage of a special type of function we have not seen before called a constructor function.

The first line of this function declares a function called **E**:

```
function E(){};
```

By convention constructor functions always start with a capital letter. This is because there is nothing different between a regular function, a method, and a constructor function except (you guessed it) the meaning of the special **this** variable, and the fact that a constructor function implicitly returns a new object.

On the next line, we set the prototype for the **E** constructor function:

```
E.prototype = obj;
```

This means that anytime we use the **E** constructor function to create a new object, it will implicitly set the passed in object to be its prototype, and therefore it will have access to all the functionality defined in that prototype.

Constructor functions are the closest JavaScript has to classes. They must be called with the **new** keyword, and as a result will construct an object that is implicitly returned when the constructor finishes. Before finishing our look at the **extends** function, it is worth learning a little more about constructor functions.

Within a constructor function you can use the special **this** variable to set properties on the implicitly created object. For instance, if we had written the following constructor function:

```
> function Person(firstName, lastName) {
    this.firstName = firstName;
    this.lastName = lastName;
}
```

you could then construct a person as follows:

```
> p = new Person('John', 'Smith');
```

The constructor implicitly returns the newly created object even though it has no return statement. This **p** variable will therefore contain a reference to an object with the appropriate name properties set.

If you omit the **new** keyword when calling a constructor function, it will act like any other function. This is why constructor functions start with a capital letter by default: to remind you to add the **new** keyword.

Omitting the **new** keyword is actually far worse than it may look. Inside the constructor function you have access to a **this** variable that refers to the newly constructed object. If you omit the **new** keyword **this** will refer to what it does in normal functions: the **window** object.

> The **window** object is a global object within the browser that contains information about the document. When JavaScript is used outside the browser an alternative global object is provided in place of **window**.

This is a huge source of bugs because the code appears to work, but all instances of the class will overwrite the same variables in the global namespace.

```
> p = Person('John', 'Smith');
```

The value of **p** is now **undefined**, since the function does not have a return value, but the **window** object has had two new properties added to it:

```
> window.firstName
```

```
John
```

```
> window.lastName
```

```
Smith
```

This is one of the reasons I recommend against constructor functions except in controlled environments such as the **extends** function.

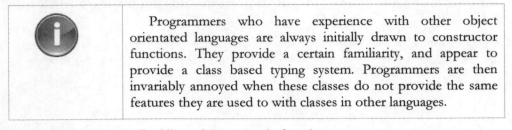

Programmers who have experience with other object orientated languages are always initially drawn to constructor functions. They provide a certain familiarity, and appear to provide a class based typing system. Programmers are then invariably annoyed when these classes do not provide the same features they are used to with classes in other languages.

Finally, we can look at the final line of the **extends** function:

return new E();

This is simply returning a new object created by the **E** constructor. Since we only need to write the **extends** function once however, we will not forget the **new** keyword.

You can now use the **extends** function to create some objects:

```
> p1 = extend(person)

> p1.firstName = 'John'

> p1.lastName = 'Smith'

> p1.age = 34
```

As the examples above illustrate, semi colons are actually optional in JavaScript. It is highly recommended that all statements are terminated with semi-colons however, since JavaScript will automatically add them when they are missing, and in some cases they will not be added where they are expected. This is another common source of hard to find bugs, for instance, the following function returns **undefined**:

```
function a() {
    return
        {a:1};
}
```

Once the instance is populated with the appropriate properties, you can use the methods defined on the prototype:

```
> p1.getFullName()
```

```
"John Smith"
```

Notice that the references to **this** inside the prototype now refer to the object itself and the full name of the person is returned.

JavaScript is a type of object orientated language called a "prototype-based language". Prototype languages use existing objects as the basis for new objects, which are then modified to meet their specific needs. The fact that JavaScript also supports syntax for creating Class-like structures sometimes obscures this fact.

Prototype-based languages look unfamiliar to most people who have used other classical object orientated languages such as C++ or Java. The approach is very powerful however, and the examples in this book will favor prototypes to classes as the basic approach to code reuse.

Prototype-based object orientated languages are relatively rare, which is why they are so unfamiliar. Other than languages based on JavaScript, it is unlikely most software engineers will ever encounter another prototype-based language. In order to succeed with JavaScript it is important to be aware of its fundamental nature however, and embrace it rather than fight it.

Functional Programming

Understanding JavaScript begins with the realization that it is a prototype-based object orientated language. The next phase in understanding JavaScript comes from realizing that it is also a functional-orientated programming language.

 There is no standard definition for what makes a programming language a "functional programming language". This section will highlight the aspects of JavaScript that make it a functional programming language without addressing arguments against considering it a functional language.

JavaScript has first class functions. This means variables can contain references to functions, and functions can be passed as arguments to other functions.

The following is an example of assigning a function to a variable:

```
> f = function() {
    console.log('Hello World');
    }
```

The variable **f** now contains a reference to a function. If we execute:

```
> typeof f
```

The result will be

```
"function"
```

Strictly speaking this is incorrect: functions are objects, and have methods just like other objects. As we saw earlier, functions are not considered a distinct data type.

Following this precedence, you may expect that the **typeof** an array would be **array**: it is not, it will return **object**.

Once you have a reference to a function, you can execute it by appending () to its name:

```
> f()
```

Hello World

First class functions are a powerful concept. As another example, consider this as a stand-alone function assigned to a variable:

```
> f2 = function(i) {
        return i % 2 == 0;
    }
```

This function accepts a number, and returns true if the number is even, and false if it is odd:

```
> f2(9)
```

```
false
```

```
> f2(10)
```

```
true
```

Now, create an array of all the numbers between 1 and 10, and assign that to variable **a**:

```
a = [1,2,3,4,5,6,7,8,9,10]
```

As mentioned earlier, JavaScript arrays are objects, and therefore they contain methods. One of the methods supported by arrays is **filter**. This method accepts a function as a parameter; the **filter** method will then pass each member of the array in turn to the function provided, and at the end return a new array containing each value that evaluated to true in that function. This means we can create a new array with all the even numbers as follows:

```
> a.filter(f2)
```

```
[2, 4, 6, 8, 10]
```

 The **filter**, **map** and **reduce** methods referred to in these examples were only added to JavaScript in ECMAScript version 5. As such they are not natively supported in older browsers, including IE8. They can however easily be added as polyfills.

Of course, we did not need to declare the function first, we could have written the same functionality as follows:

```
> a.filter(function(i) {return i % 2 == 0})
```

```
[2, 4, 6, 8, 10]
```

The function passed to the **filter** method in this case is an anonymous function (i.e. a function without a name). This function only exists for the duration of the filter call, and cannot be reused.

Let's now imagine a more complex example. Suppose we want to take an array, multiply each element by itself, and then return the result if it is even.

JavaScript arrays also have a method called **map**. Like **filter**, **map** passes each member of the array to a function, and then returns a new array with the result of these function calls.

It is important to note that these methods are not altering the original array; they are creating a new array with the appropriate entries. This is an important paradigm, since it means the method call will not impact any other code that has a reference to the original array.

In order to multiply each member by itself, we could execute:

```
> a.map(function(i) {return i*i})
```

```
[1, 4, 9, 16, 25, 36, 49, 64, 81, 100]
```

In order to return the even numbers amongst these, we could therefore perform the **filter** method on the array returned by the **map** call:

```
a.map(function(i) {return i*i}).filter(function(i) {return i % 2 == 0})
```

```
[4, 16, 36, 64, 100]
```

Finally, let's imagine that we want to sum the values in the final array. **Arrays.prototype** supports a **reduce** method for this. This method is slightly more complex than **map** and **filter**, since the method must keep track of the current count. This method will pass the following to our function for each member in the array:

1. The current result.

2. The value of the current member of the array.

3. The index that member has in the array (starting at 0).

4. The array itself.

The methods **filter**, **map** and **reduce** are not unique to JavaScript. These are important operators for dealing with data sets in many languages, and were popularised by Google's map/reduce algorithm for indexing web pages.

http://static.googleusercontent.com/external_content/untru sted_dlcp/research.google.com/en//archive/mapreduce-osdi04.pdf

In order to see this working, execute the following:

```
[1,2,3,4,5].reduce(function(total, currentValue, index, array) {
    console.log('Current value is ' + currentValue);
    console.log('Total is ' + total);
    return total += currentValue;
});
```

This will print the following:

```
Current value is 2


Total is 1


Current value is 3


Total is 3


Current value is 4


Total is 6


Current value is 5


Total is 10


15
```

The total value is initially set to the value of the first element in the array. Each member is then passed to the function, and we add this to the total. At the end, the total is 15, which is returned from the **reduce** method.

We can now write our final version of the code with **map**, **filter** and **reduce** chained together, each using the result of its predecessor as its input:

```
> a.map(function(i) {return i*i})
   .filter(function(i) {return i % 2 == 0})
   .reduce(function(total, currentValue, index, array) {
        return total += currentValue;
   })
```

220

Functions that accept other functions allow software engineers to write extremely concise code. In many strongly typed Object Orientated languages, such as Java, functions are not first class language constructs (although Java 8 has introduced lambda expressions, which serve essentially the same purpose). In order to write a function (or method), you first must construct a class to contain it, and then an object from that class.

Function Arguments

JavaScript does not check that the arguments passed to a function match the signature of the function. For instance:

- You can pass more arguments to a function than it expects; in this case the extra arguments will be ignored.

- You can pass fewer arguments to a function than it expects; in this case the arguments are assigned the value of **undefined**.

> A side effect of this is that it is not possible to overload functions or methods in JavaScript. In many languages it is possible to define multiple versions of the same function, but with different parameter lists (or signatures). The compiler then determines the correct version to invoke based on the parameters provided.
>
> In order to achieve this in JavaScript the functions must be given different names, otherwise JavaScript cannot determine the correct version to invoke.

There are legitimate reasons to pass fewer arguments to a function than it expects. You may be happy for these arguments to be **undefined**.

There are also legitimate reasons to pass more arguments to a function than its signature specifies. For instance, consider a function that accepts an arbitrary number of arguments, and adds them all together.

Any time a function is invoked a variable called **arguments** is available inside the function. This is an array containing all the variables passed to the function. This means we can defined an **add** function as a function that accepts no parameters, but instead uses the **arguments** array:

```
> function add() {
    var result = 0;
    for (var i = 0; i < arguments.length; i++) {
        result += arguments[i];
    }
    return result;
}
```

This function uses a standard for-loop to iterate through all the arguments, and simply adds them to a **result** variable that is returned at the end.

This can then be invoked as follows:

```
> add(6,2,9,20)
```

37

Naturally, it is especially important to add comments to functions that accept variable numbers of parameters; otherwise it can be difficult to work out how to invoke them.

Closures

Closures are another of the most important features of JavaScript. When we continue the development of the sample web application we will make extensive use of closures.

Closures can be a difficult concept to explain, so it is useful to learn about them through examples.

Consider the following code:

```
> function f() {
    var i = 0;
    return ++i;
}
```

 This example uses ++i rather than i++. This means that the value is incremented (has 1 added to it with the ++ operator) before it is returned. If this had used i++, the value would be returned and then incremented by 1 – which is not the same thing.

This code defines a function **f**. Inside this function a private variable is declared and initialized to 0. This variable is then incremented by 1 and returned.

If we perform repeated calls to this function, it is not surprising that it will always return 1:

```
> f()
```

```
1
```

```
> f()
```

```
1
```

```
> f()
```

```
1
```

Each time this function is executed it declares a new variable, which is scoped to the function. The keyword **var** is used to indicate that the variable is function scoped rather than global scoped. The newly created variable has 1 added to it, and the value is returned. When the function ends the variable is destroyed.

If we try to access the variable **i** outside the function an error will be generated:

```
> i
```

```
ReferenceError: i is not defined
```

The error is not because the variable is being accessed outside the function; it is because it does not exist anymore. Function variables are placed on a stack when the function begins execution, and when the function completes they are popped off the stack and destroyed.

Programming languages use this approach for good reason. This ensures the space allocated to variables inside functions is automatically reclaimed when the function completes. This guards against out of memory errors.

On the face of it this all seems to make sense. There are however good reasons why we may wish to access function scoped variables even after functions complete. We do not however want to make these variables global variables (as we could do by omitting the **var** keyword on the variable declaration). This can be achieved via closures.

Consider the following code:

```
> function f2() {
    var i = 0;
    return function() {
        return ++i;
    };
}
```

This function does the following:

1. Declares a function scoped variable called **i** initialized to the value 0.

2. Returns a function that will increment this variable when invoked.

We can therefore call this function and assign the result (which is a function) to a variable:

```
> incrementer = f2()
```

Based on our explanation of function scoped variables above, you would expect that the variable declared inside **f2** would be destroyed when the function call **f2** completed. Therefore, when we invoke the function that was returned from **f2**, there would be no **i** variable for it to access (since it has been destroyed). This is not the case:

```
> incrementer()
```

```
1
```

```
> incrementer()
```

```
2
```

```
> incrementer()
```

```
3
```

When the anonymous function was defined inside function **f2** it "closed" over its environment as it existed at that point of time, and kept a copy of that environment. Since the variable **i** was accessible when the function was declared, it is still available when the function is invoked. JavaScript has realized that the anonymous function refers to the variable **i**, and that this function has not been destroyed, and therefore it has not destroyed the **i** variable it depends on.

If we construct another function using the same mechanism:

```
> incrementer2 = f2()
```

This will also have access to a variable called **i** as it existed when the function was created, but it will be a new version of that variable:

```
> incrementer2()
```

```
1
```

```
> incrementer2()
```

```
2
```

```
> incrementer2()
```

3

This may look like a simple quirk of the language, but it is an incredibly powerful feature.

JavaScript by default is not very good at hiding data. It is not possible to declare properties as private inside an object. For instance, consider the following object that provides the same basic "incrementer" functionality:

```
> obj1 = {i: 0,
  increment: function() {
    return ++this.i;
  }
}
```

This appears to work correctly:

```
> obj1.increment()
```

1

```
> obj1.increment()
```

2

```
> obj1.increment()
```

3

There is a potential problem here though. Anyone with a reference to this object can change the current value of **i**:

```
> obj1.i = 20
```

Once this is done, with the next call to increment, the number will jump to 21:

```
> obj1.increment()
```

21

This may be a big problem; it may be an even bigger problem if the following occurs:

```
> obj1.i = "hello world"
```

Now the next call will return the following:

```
> obj1.increment()
```

NaN

The closure-based implementation solves this problem. There is no way to modify the value of **i**, or impact the value returned by the function. If a call to the function returns 5, the next call to the function is guaranteed to return 6.

Data hiding (or encapsulation) is an enormously important concept when writing large applications. It allows us to write code modules with well-defined public interfaces (or APIs), while hiding (or encapsulating) the internal logic and state from the caller. This reduces bugs, since code cannot accidentally corrupt the state of the module.

The approach used to implement the closure-based **incrementer** is a representation of a design pattern. A design pattern is a commonly used, reusable approach to solving a common problem. This approach is referred to as the **module** design pattern.

The module design pattern is also commonly implemented by returning an object rather than a function. This allows the object to use private variables for its private properties and functions, while still exposing a series of public properties and methods. The functionality above can be rewritten as follows:

```
> function createIncrementer() {
    var i = 0;
    return {
        increment: function() {
            return ++i;
        }
    };
}
```

We can now create an **incremeter** object:

```
> obj2 = createIncrementer();
```

Once created, we now call the increment method, and consistently receive a value incremented by 1:

```
> obj2.increment()


1


> obj2.increment()


2


> obj2.increment()
```

3

We can attempt to change the internal state of the object by calling the following:

```
> obj2.i = 10
```

but all this will do is create a new property on the object:

```
> obj2.i
```

10

This is not the same variable that is being used as the incrementing state of the object:

```
> obj2.increment()
```

4

```
> obj2.increment()
```

5

```
> obj2.increment()
```

6

Scope and "this"

In order to fully understand a language, you must understand its approach to scoping variables. Understanding scope tells us when various variables are available within the program, and which variable is used if there are multiple variables available with the same name.

Let's start with a simple example:

```
> function getNumber() {
        num = 10;
        return num;
  }
```

This is a function that always returns the same number: 10.

```
> getNumber()
```

```
10
```

```
> getNumber()
```

```
10
```

When this function finishes execution, it may seem that the variable **num** would no longer be available based on our discussion of function scoped variables earlier in this chapter. This is not the case:

```
> num
```

```
10
```

This is because we forgot to use **var** when declaring the variable. If we had done the following, the variable would not have existed after the function completed:

```
> function getNumber() {

      var num = 10;

      return num;

  }
```

Due to the fact **var** was omitted; the **num** variable was added as a property to the object represented by a special variable called **this**. Within a function, **this** refers to a special object called **window**. You can see this by typing **this** in the console:

```
> this
```

```
Window {top: Window, window: Window, location: Location, external: Obje
ct, chrome: Object…}
```

 Strictly speaking this is not true: it is only true of functions executed in a browser environment. JavaScript written in server side applications will use a different object than **window** for the global scope.

In fact, this function could have been written as follows:

```
> function getNumber() {

      this.num = 10;

      return this.num;

  }
```

The **window** object is a global object that contains information about the browser environment, but is also the object that properties are added to by default within functions. The **window** object is available to any code in the web page (including external libraries), and therefore it is referred to as the global scope.

Adding properties to the **window** object is dangerous in any moderately sized application. Since the global properties can be read and written by any piece of code, there is a significant possibility that other code will accidentally overwrite your variables.

> If you do need to create global variables (and the sample application will create a couple), it is often a good idea to create a single object on the **window** to hold all the variables for your application:
>
> ```
> > window.THEAPP = {};
> > window.THEAPP.myproperty = 'myvalue ';
> ```

As mentioned earlier, the **this** variable takes on a different meaning inside an object's method:

```
> obj = { num: 10,
    add: function(num2) {
      this.num += num2;
      return this.num;
    }
}
```

This is a very simple object that contains a **num** property initialized to 10. It also exposes an **add** method that adds the parameter passed in to this property and returns the result:

```
> obj.add(10)
```

20

```
> obj.add(10)
```

30

You will notice that **this** inside an object method refers not to the global **window** object, but to the object itself.

Let's take this one step further:

```
> obj = { num: 10,
    add: function(num2) {
      helper = function(num2) {
        this.num += num2;
        return this.num;
```

```
    }
    return helper(num2);
  }
}
```

In this example we are declaring a function inside the object's method. Although this is a contrived example, the approach used here is common (especially for event listeners).

Intuitively it looks like this code should work: the helper function is using **this.num** to access the **num** property on the object. Unfortunately this code does not work as expected:

```
> obj.add(20)

NaN
```

The problem can be seen if we add some logging to the code:

```
> obj = { nums: 10,
    add: function(num2) {
      console.log('Outer this ' + this)
      helper = function(num2) {
        console.log('Inner this ' + this)
        this.num += num2;
        return this.num;
      }
      return helper(num2);
    }
  }
```

If you execute this now, you will see the following output:

```
> obj.add(20)

Outer this [object Object]
Inner this [object Window]
NaN
```

Surprisingly the **this** inside the inner function has reverted from being the object to being the **window**. This is considered by most as a bug in the language, but it is a bug that will not be rectified since it would break legacy code.

The common way to avoid this issue is as follows:

```
> obj = { num: 10,
    add: function(num2) {
```

```
    var that = this;
    helper = function(num2) {
    that.num += num2;
    return that.num;
  }
    return helper(num2);
  }
}
```

Before entering the inner function we declare a variable called **that**, and set it to refer to the **this** object (the object itself). Inside the inner function we then access the **that** variable rather than the **this** variable.

So far we have seen two different definitions of the **this** variable. In both these cases **this** was implicitly defined by the programming environment. It is also possible to explicitly specify the object that should be used to represent **this**. In order to see this in action we will define a new object that adds two properties together:

```
> adder = {
  num1: 10,
  num2: 20,
  add: function() {
    return this.num1+this.num2;
  }
}
```

If we call the **add** method, the two properties will be added together and returned:

```
> adder.add()
```

30

As mentioned earlier, functions and methods are actually objects in JavaScript, and therefore they support their own methods. These are defined on **Function.prototype**, (so naturally you can also add your own methods to functions). One of the methods **Function.prototype** supports is **apply**, which allows an alternative environment to be provided for the **this** variable:

```
> adder.add.apply({num1:30,num2:40})
```

70

The parameter passed to **apply** is an object containing the appropriate properties required by the function. This approach can be used to replace the value of **this** in standalone functions and object methods.

Another method provided to **Function.prototype** is **bind**. Rather than executing the function using the object passed in as the environment, **bind** returns a new function that permanently binds the object passed in as the **this** variable for the function:

```
> add2 = adder.add.bind({num1:30,num2:40})
```

It is now possible to execute the function as follows:

```
> add2()
```

70

We can use this method to solve the problem we encountered with inner functions in this example:

```
> obj = { nums: 10,
    add: function(num2) {
        console.log('Outer this ' + this)
        helper = function(num2) {
        console.log('Inner this ' + this)
        this.num += num2;
          return this.num;

      }
      return helper(num2);
    }
}
```

This can be rewritten as follows:

```
> obj = { num: 10,
      add: function(num2) {
        console.log('Outer this ' + this)
        helper = function(num2) {
          console.log('Inner this ' + this)
          this.num += num2;
          return this.num;
        }.bind(this);
      return helper(num2);
    }
}
```

Executing this now produces the correct result:

```
> obj.add(20)
```

```
Outer this [object Object]
Inner this [object Object]
30
```

Earlier in this book I mentioned a fourth way **this** could be defined: inside constructor functions. Within a constructor function **this** refers to the implicitly created object, provided the function was invoked with the **new** modifier. Without the **new** modifier, **this** becomes the global object again.

It is worth mentioning one more limitation of JavaScript before completing this section. JavaScript does not support block level scope. This can be seen in the following example:

```
function test() {
    var a = [1,2,3,4];
    for (var i = 0; i < a.length; i++) {
        var a = i;
        console.log(a);
    }
    console.log(a);
}
```

The inner block here uses the same variable name **a** as is used in the outer block. In most programing languages the two variables named **a** would be different, because they are defined in different blocks of code. JavaScript does not support block level scoping: it only supports function level scoping, therefore the line:

```
var a = i;
```

overwrites the variable defined here:

```
var a = [1,2,3,4];
```

In addition to being limited to function-level scoping, JavaScript employs another technique for all the variables defined within a function called "hoisting". Before explaining "hoisting", try to work out why only one of these two functions produces an error when executed:

```
> function testLocal() {
    console.log(j);
    var j = 10;
}
```

```
> function testGlobal() {
    console.log(j);
```

```
    j = 10;
}
```

Intuitively it looks like both of these functions will fail because they are attempting to access a variable before it is declared. In fact, when JavaScript functions are executed they first look for all function scoped variables that will be declared anywhere in the function. These are then "hoisted" to the top of the function.

These function variables remain undefined until explicitly assigned a value, but they do exist as undefined variables. Globally defined variables are not hoisted, and therefore the two functions produce different results:

```
> testLocal()


undefined


> testGlobal()


ReferenceError: j is not defined
```

For this reason it is always best practice to declare function scoped variables at the top of the function, since this is what the language will automatically do anyway.

Exception Handling

We will discuss approaches to implementing application wide exception handling later in this book. For now, it is worth emphasizing that JavaScript does support "Java-style" exception handling, but without the benefits provided by static typing.

Any code can throw an exception without declaring that it will throw that exception. Any data type can be thrown as an exception, although it is common practice to throw an object with a code and a message. This function throws an exception if it is passed an even number:

```
> function dontLikeEven(num) {
    if (num % 2 == 0) {
        throw {code: 'even_number',
        message: 'This function cannot be called with even numbers'
        };
    }
}
```

It is also possible to catch an exception, and provide logic to handle the failure scenario:

```
> function passNumber(num) {
  try {
      dontLikeEven(num);
```

```
} catch(e) {
  console.log(e.code+':'+e.message);
  console.log('Retying with ' + (num+1));
  dontLikeEven(num+1);
}
}
```

In order to catch exceptions, a **try** block must be declared in the code. Only errors that occur in this block will be caught. A **catch** block must be provided at the end of the **try** block, and this will be passed any exception that occurs in the block.

The function above produces the following output if it is invoked with an even number:

```
> passNumber(2)


even_number:This function cannot be called with even numbers
Retying with 3
```

Unlike Java, only a single **catch** block can be provided, and this block must then determine the cause of the exception. If required the **catch** block can throw another exception.

Try/catch blocks should be provided to catch application logic exceptions, not to hide coding bugs. We will explore this topic further later in the book.

Threading

Unlike most languages, JavaScript does not offer programmers an approach for utilizing multiple threads.

Within the browser environment, all JavaScript code executes on a single thread, and this is also the thread that the browser utilizes to update the window. This means that if you make changes to the DOM, and then continue to utilize the thread to perform any computation, your DOM changes will not be applied until you finish this processing.

Browsers do allow documents in different tabs to utilize different threads: this is possible because the tabs do not interact with one another.

The browser manages the single thread with an event queue. Each time an event occurs, be it a browser initiated event such as resizing the window, a user initiated even such as clicking a button, or a JavaScript initiated event such as a timer executing a function, the event is added to a queue. The browser then processes these events sequentially and does not begin processing a new event until all the events ahead of it have finished processing.

This threading model can cause issues, since it does not prioritize the processing of events based on their source. In real-world applications it is often more important to respond to user based events quickly, even if that means temporarily interrupting a computational process currently executing.

HTML5 has addressed this issue to a degree with an API called Web Workers. These will be introduced later in the book, but they are not a general purpose solution to threading issues, since they contain numerous limitations.

JavaScript does provide a mechanism to alleviate some of the issues inherent in the single thread model with the **setTimeout** function defined in the language. The **setTimeout** function allows code to execute at a delayed interval.

In order to see **setTimeout** in action, we will first define a function that we wish to execute at a delayed interval:

```
> writer = function() {
  for (var i = 0; i < 10; i++) {
    console.log('Row '+i);
  }
}
```

Next we will ask the browser thread to execute this with a delay of 5000 milliseconds:

```
> setTimeout(writer, 5000)
```

If you execute this you should see the execution begin after approximately 5 seconds. JavaScript executes this by encapsulated the function call in an event and adding that event to the event queue after 5 seconds. It will then still only execute when it gets to the front of the event queue.

Before performing a long running calculation, it is sometimes useful to yield control back to the browser to ensure any other events that are waiting can be processed (particularly user driven events) first, and therefore stop the application from appearing to "lock-up".

Your processing can be encapsulated in a call to **setTimeout** with a very small delay (10 milliseconds for instance). This will guarantee that you go to the back of the event queue (and any pending events will occur first), but still will not result in any unnecessary delay if there are no other events waiting to run.

The **setTimeout** function can also be used to yield control back to the browser during a long running task. If you were to perform a computation that took 10 seconds, by default you would not be interrupted during this period, so all other events would queue up behind you. Instead, if there is a way of breaking the computation up, you can choose a point where you wish to yield, and ask the next portion of the algorithm to run by calling **setTimeout** with a delay of 10 milliseconds.

If this was done every 100 milliseconds, it is unlikely the user would notice that there was a long running computational process executing on the same thread.

The main challenge in achieving this is pausing and resuming the computation. It will typically be necessary to store the current state of the algorithm, and pass this to the function that will continue the processing.

setTimeout has a companion function called **setInterval**. Unlike **setTimeout** which causes a function to be executed once, **setInterval** causes a function to be executed indefinitely with a given delay between executions. The following is a simple example:

```
> setInterval(function() {
    console.log('hello world');
  }, 1000)
```

This will cause "hello world" to be printed to the console indefinitely every second. **setInterval** is very useful for implementing background jobs that need to perform operations periodically.

As with **setTimeout**, **setInterval** generates events that are placed on the event queue. Therefore they can only run once they get to the front of the event queue.

Although **setTimeout** and **setInterval** are rudimentary compared to the threading libraries common in most programming languages, it is important to have a strong grasp of what they do, and when you should use them. They do allow many of the issues associated with the single thread model (particularly unresponsive GUIs, and slow reactions to user events) to be alleviated.

Conclusion

JavaScript is best described as a multi-paradigm language: it supports the following programming paradigms:

- Functional programming

- Imperative programming

- Classical object orientated programming

- Prototype-based programming

Due to its multi-paradigm nature, JavaScript is enormously flexible. The danger with JavaScript's multi-paradigm nature is that it allows programmers to see in it what they want, without taking into account which of these paradigms are JavaScript's true strengths.

This chapter has presented the case that JavaScript should be best thought of as a prototype-based, functional programming language.

JavaScript's approach to functions is a particular strength. First class functions are a powerful concept, and allow for concise, reusable code.

JavaScript's approach to prototyping is perhaps its least understood feature, and while unusual as a design choice in the language, is another key strength of the language.

Finally, JavaScript has more than its fair share of quirks and design bugs. The key to circumventing these is to understand they exist. These quirks can be easily worked around by those who understand them, but can cause annoying bugs for those who don't.

6 JQUERY

Understanding jQuery begins with an understanding of JavaScript. Sometimes jQuery is treated as an independent language that can be used instead of JavaScript. Although jQuery contains many features associated with programming languages, it is best thought of as a library that enhances JavaScript in specific situations. For this reason, JavaScript has been introduced before jQuery.

Before understanding jQuery however, it is worth taking a brief look at the Document Object Model (DOM), since jQuery is primarily a library for dealing with the DOM in a browser independent manner.

Document Object Model

HTML (including XML and XHTML) documents are modeled in memory using a tree structure called the Document Object Model.

Each document has a single parent node, and this node can have children. These nodes in turn can be parents of other children. Each node in the tree (except the head node) has one, and only one parent. All nodes in the tree can have zero or more children.

DOM trees contain several kinds of node, the most common of which are element nodes (which represent tags) and text nodes (which represent the content inside tags).

In order to see the inherent tree structure of a document, open the tasks.html document from chapter 4, and view it in the "Elements" tab of Chrome's developer tools. Any parent that has children has an arrow beside it that can be expanded. The overall parent of the whole document is the **html** tag at the start of the document. This has two children: **head** and **body**, and each of these have children. Even in this relatively simple document, there are some elements that are eight generations removed from the **html** element:

```
×   Elements  Resources  Network  Sources  Timeline  Profiles  Audits  Console
<!DOCTYPE html>
▼ <html lang="en">
  ▼ <head>
      <meta charset="utf-8">
      <title>Task list</title>
      <link rel="stylesheet" type="text/css" href="styles/tasks.css" media="screen">
    </head>
  ▼ <body>
    ▶ <header>…</header>
    ▼ <main>
      ▼ <section>
        ▼ <form>
          ▼ <div>
              <label>Task</label>
              <input type="text" required="required" name="task" class="large" placeholder="Bre
            </div>
          ▼ <div>
              <label>Required by</label>
              <input type="date" required="required" name="requiredBy">
            </div>
          ▼ <div>
              <label>Category</label>
            ▼ <select name="category">
                <option value="Personal">Personal</option>
                <option value="Work">Work</option>
              </select>
            </div>
          ▼ <nav>
              <a href="#">Save task</a>
              <a href="#">Clear task</a>
            </nav>
          </form>
        </section>
      ▼ <section>
        ▼ <table>
          ▼ <colgroup>
              <col width="50%">
              <col width="25%">
              <col width="25%">
            </colgroup>
          ▼ <thead>
            ▼ <tr>
                <th>Name</th>
                <th>Due</th>
                <th>Category</th>
              </tr>
            </thead>
          ▼ <tbody>
            ▼ <tr>
                <td>Return library books</td>
              ▼ <td>
                  <time datetime="2013-10-14">2013-10-14</time>
                </td>
```

The Document Object Model is a technology and language independent API for interacting with HTML documents. The API allows developers to access nodes in the document, traverse the document, and manipulate elements in the document.

Each element in the DOM tree is represented by an object. These objects support an API that allows them to be manipulated. As you will see when we start using jQuery; sometimes we will still encounter native DOM objects, but usually they will be wrapped inside jQuery specific versions of the objects, and expose additional functionality.

All web browsers that support JavaScript support a JavaScript implementation of the DOM API. The specific version of the API they support will depend on the browser however, and this, along with inconsistencies in their implementations, can lead to issues for JavaScript programmers.

In order to see the DOM API in action, open the Chrome console and type the following:

```
> document
```

This will return the DOM representation of the HTML document, which is the exact same representation we saw from the Elements tab of the developer tools above. This may differ from the literal document: for instance if the HTML document was not well formed (e.g. it was missing closing tags), the browser will attempt to construct a well-formed representation of the document (according to the rules specified in the HTML5 specification).

The DOM API allows us to access elements based on their characteristics; for instance, we can access the **table** elements with:

```
> document.getElementsByTagName('table')
```

In addition to querying, traversing and manipulating the document, the DOM API also allows event listeners to be added to the nodes in the document. These can be used to detect users clicking buttons, or text being typed into input fields, along with many other types of event.

jQuery does not allow you to do anything with the DOM that could not be done using the native JavaScript API, in fact, jQuery is implemented using the native DOM API, and is therefore essentially an abstraction or wrapper of the DOM API.

Since jQuery does not do anything that cannot be done with the native DOM API you may wonder what is the use of learning jQuery. For one thing, jQuery provides a genuine cross browser implementation of the DOM API, and alleviates the quirks that are found in many browser implementations.

Rather than providing a full set of reasons for using jQuery, I encourage you to work through the examples below. They highlight the elegance and conciseness of the jQuery API, and once you begin using jQuery it is very hard to go back to the native DOM API.

Starting with jQuery

In order to use jQuery you must include the jQuery library in the HTML page. This can be achieved by serving your own copy of the jQuery library, or by utilizing a hosted version from a content delivery network (CDN), most notably Google.

 As a general rule, for production deployment you should favour CDN hosted options. These tend to provide superior performance for users than hosting your own copy. For development I generally prefer to download my own copy, since this removes the need for a network connection to run the

application.

If you wish to use the Google hosted version of jQuery, simply include it in the head of the HTML file:

```
<script
src="http://ajax.googleapis.com/ajax/libs/jquery/2.0.3/jquery.min.js"><
/script>
```

In order to serve your own copy, download the latest version of jQuery from here:

http://jquery.com/download/

The examples in this book are using 2.0.3, but any recent version will be compatible.

jQuery consists of a single JavaScript file that can be downloaded in either minimized or non-minimalized form. The non-minimalized form is useful for debugging, but either version will be appropriate. Once downloaded, save the file in a subdirectory of the main folder (the one containing the HTML file) called "scripts".

Your directory structure should now look like this:

▼ 🗂 scripts
      📄 jquery-2.0.3.js
▼ 🗂 styles
      📄 tasks.css
  📄 tasks.html

Now add the following to the head section of the HTML file:

```
<script src="scripts/jquery-2.0.3.js"></script>
```

In order to verify you have performed these steps correctly, open the page, and open the JavaScript console. Type the following into the console:

```
> jQuery
```

If this does not generate an error, jQuery is ready to go.

Selection

The first thing we are going to do with jQuery is select elements from the document.

Selecting elements obviously has no intrinsic value in its own right; we are eventually going to do something with these elements. A jQuery selection will return zero or more elements from the document. More specifically, the selection will return zero or more jQuery wrapped DOM elements from the document. This distinction will be important in later sections.

In order to perform a selection, simply include the selection criteria inside the following construct:

```
$('<selection criteria>')
```

The **$** is an alias for the function called jQuery, so we could also use the following construct:

```
jQuery('<selection criteria>')
```

The **$** alias tends to produce better readability, so we will use that convention in the sections below. The only time to avoid this alias is if you are using any other libraries that use the **$** global variable: jQuery does support a no-conflicts mode in this case, and allows you to create a new alias.

The selection criteria utilized by jQuery is in fact essentially the same selection criteria utilized by CSS. This is enormously helpful, since it means you only need to learn the selection language once in order to use CSS and jQuery.

There are five core ways to select elements:

- Element type.

- Element attribute.

- Element class.

- Element ID.

- Pseudo classes.

All five approaches will be briefly outlined below.

The first way to select an element is by its type. For instance, if we want to select all the **table** elements in the document, we can use the following syntax:

```
> $('table')
```

This, and all other commands in this chapter, can be run directly in the console after first loading the tasks.html page. This command will return an array of one element, and that element will be the table holding the tasks.

If we want to select all the **td** elements in a document, we can use the following:

```
> $('td')
```

This will return an array of 9 elements.

The second core way we can select elements is based on one of their attributes. If we wish to select all the elements with a placeholder attribute, the following selection can be used:

```
> $('[placeholder]')
```

Notice the use of **[]** brackets around the attribute name. This will find all elements with a placeholder attribute, regardless of its value.

Additionally, we may wish to specify that the element has an attribute with a specific value, in which case the following syntax can be used:

```
> $'[datetime="2013-10-14"]')
```

In this case we are mixing single and double quotes, since we wish to express the value as a string inside the string that is the selection criteria.

Selecting elements based on attributes becomes even more useful due to the fact it is possible to add your own custom attributes to HTML elements. Adding custom attributes to elements allows you to associate data with an element, and then use this data in any way you need.

For instance, we may want to denote that a cell in a table represents the name of a task; therefore we could add the following attribute to the element:

```
<td data-name-field="true">
```

In order to quickly find all name field nodes, we could then execute the following selection:

```
> $('[data-name-field]')
```

Alternatively, we may wish to associate a priority with tasks, so each **tr** element could include the following:

```
<tr data-priority="high">
```

or

```
<tr data-priority="medium">
```

We can then select all the high priority rows in the table with the following selection:

```
> $('[data-priority="high"]')
```

We will see below that the prefix added to this attribute ("data-") is more than a convention, and allows for other possibilities. Binding data directly to elements turns out to be an enormously powerful concept. It provides a way to add context to elements in a manner that can be easily understood and processed by code, and therefore allows the same element to have user facing and a computer facing meaning.

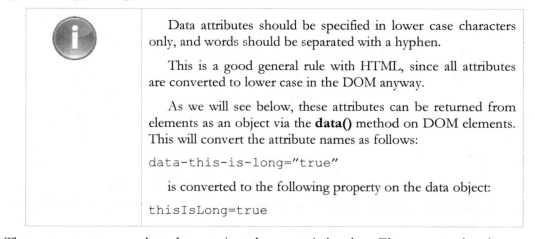

Data attributes should be specified in lower case characters only, and words should be separated with a hyphen.

This is a good general rule with HTML, since all attributes are converted to lower case in the DOM anyway.

As we will see below, these attributes can be returned from elements as an object via the **data()** method on DOM elements. This will convert the attribute names as follows:

```
data-this-is-long="true"
```

is converted to the following property on the data object:

```
thisIsLong=true
```

The next way we can select elements in a document is by class. Elements can be given one or more classes with the **class** attribute. All HTML elements support the **class** attribute (the restrictions from HTML4 applying to some elements have been removed). Inside tasks.html you will see the following examples:

```
<input type="text" required="required" name="task" class="large">

<tr class="even">
```

A class is just an arbitrary name: it is a way of grouping together otherwise unrelated elements to denote they share some characteristic. The characteristic they usually have in common is that they should have the same styles applied via CSS, and therefore the class attribute is usually associated purely with CSS.

In reality classes can be used to group elements for any reason. When using jQuery it is common to assign classes to elements purely to allow jQuery selections to efficiently find related elements.

For instance, in tasks.html every second row in the table is given the class of **even**. All even rows can be selected using the following selection criteria:

```
> $('.even')
```

(Note the "." at the start of the selection criteria)

It is possible to apply specific styles to every second row purely through CSS:

```
tr:nth-child(even) {
    background-color: #f8f8f8;
}
```

Using classes for reasons other than CSS matching does not go against the spirit of the HTML5 specification. The specification states that classes are one way that elements can be extended, thereby effectively creating a new type of element.

The fourth basic way to select elements is based on their ID. Any element can be given an ID using the **id** attribute.

ID names are arbitrary, just as class names are, but ID names must be unique within a document.

HTML5 has relaxed the rules on the values that can be used for IDs. The only rules now are that they must be unique in a document, and cannot be an empty string or contain spaces. The rules for class names are identical.

An element can be given an ID as follows:

```
<table id='tblTasks'>
```

Once an element has been given an ID it can be selected with the following criteria:

```
> $('#tblTasks')
```

(Note the "#" sign at the start of the selection criteria.)

The last way of selecting elements is via jQuery filters. If you are familiar with CSS, these may look the same as CSS pseudo-classes, and they essentially serve the same purpose.

Suppose we want to find the first row in a **table**. We could add a class to the row, but if the table was re-ordered we would need to make sure this was updated. We could also select all rows from the table into an array and choose the first element, but this is inefficient. With filters we can use the following selection criteria:

```
> $('tr:first')
```

(Filters are always prepended with a colon; this is therefore combining two selectors, one to select **tr** elements, and then another limiting the selection to **tr** elements that are in the first position amongst their siblings.)

Filters can also accept parameters; therefore we can find any arbitrary row in the table using the following filter:

```
> $('tr:eq(1)')
```

This will find the second row in the table (counting starts at 0).

Alternatively we may wish to find any row except the first row, so we could use the following filter:

```
> $('tr:gt(0)')
```

This will select all rows with a position greater than 0.

Other useful filters are as follows:

- **:even** finds all even numbered elements in a selection.

- **:odd** finds all odd numbered elements in a selection.

- **:not(selection)** finds all elements that do not match the selection.

- **:checked** finds radio buttons or check boxes that are checked.

- **:selected** finds options in select boxes that are selected.

- **:contains(text)** finds elements that contain a given piece of text.

- **:empty** finds all elements that have no children.

- **:focus** finds the element that currently has focus.

- **:last** finds the last element in a set.

In addition, filters can simplify the process of selecting input elements. Since most input fields use the element type of **input**, it is necessary to also query on the attribute **type**. jQuery contains the following filters for finding specific types of input field:

- :hidden

- :text

- :checkbox

- :password

- :radio

- :checkbox

- :file

- :button

for instance, this selects all **text** input fields:

```
> $(':text')
```

One of the nice features about jQuery filters is that you can actually write your own. For instance, jQuery does not provide a filter for finding all the **date** input types. We can therefore add a custom filter to our code-base as follows:

```
> jQuery.expr[':'].date = function(elem) {
        return jQuery(elem).is("input") && $(elem).attr("type") ===
"date";
 }
```

(Don't worry if this code looks unfamiliar, it will look familiar by the end of the chapter.)

When executed, this will be passed all elements in the document (or the specified sub-tree of the document we are realing with), and returns true or false depending on whether the specified element meets the selection criteria. The result to the caller is all the elements that evaluated to true.

 This function takes advantage of the jQuery **is** function. The **is** function is slightly unusual in that it returns **true** or **false** rather than a set of elements.

Once this has been added to the code-base, the following pseudo class can be used:

```
> $(':date')
```

Now that we have investigated the five main selection mechanisms, the next step is to understand how these mechanisms can be combined. We have already been briefly introduced to this concept with pseudo-classes.

The simplest way of combining filters is in cases where elements need to meet two or more selection criteria. For instance, if the **:text** filter did not exist, it could be written through the combination of two selection criteria. In the first instance, we would need to make sure the element was of type **input**:

```
> $('input')
```

Additionally, the element must have an attribute called **type** set to the value **text**:

```
> $('[type="text"]')
```

In order to join these two criteria, a single selection criterion can be written as follows:

```
> $('input[type="text"]')
```

Notice that there is no space between one criteria and the next – if a space was placed here this would mean something different, as we will see below.

We can use the same approach to match on both element **type** and **class**:

```
> $('input.large')
```

This will return all elements of **type** "input" that have a **class** of "large".

It should never be necessary to combine selectors based on ID with other types of selector, since IDs are unique within a document.

In addition to combining selectors for criterion relating to a single element, it is often necessary to select all elements that match selection criteria within a particular sub-tree of the document.

Consider a case where we have multiple tables in the same document, but we want to return the first row in a specific table (for instance, the table with the ID **tblTasks**). In order to achieve this we first need to find the table called **tblTasks**, and then find the first row within its sub-tree.

jQuery supports several ways of doing this. The most common approach is as follows:

```
> $('#tblTasks tr:first')
```

The space denotes the fact that these are two different selections. jQuery effectively performs this by selecting the elements that match the first selection:

```
$('#tblTasks')
```

and then executing the second selection against the sub-trees of these elements:

```
$('tr:first')
```

In fact, jQuery supports an alternative mechanism for doing this more explicitly:

```
> $('#tblTasks').find('tr:first')
```

Yet another approach to performing this same selection is to use the optional second parameter to the jQuery selector:

```
> $('tr:first', '#tblTasks')
```

The second parameter is used to specify the root of the sub-tree that the selection should occur within. This can be a useful approach when you know you are dealing with a sub-tree of the document, since you can assign the context to a variable, and then use that in all selections:

```
> documentContext = $('#tblTasks');
> $('tr:first()', documentContext);
```

It is possible to specify more than two levels of selection within a single selection criterion. For instance, we may want to find all the **td** elements in the last row of all the **tables** in the second **section** of the document. This can be performed as follows:

```
> $('section:eq(1) table tr:last td')
```

Sometimes we may want to be more precise about the relationship between elements. For instance, we may want to select elements that are direct children (rather than just decedents) of another element. This can be accomplished through the use of the ">" sign, for instance:

```
> $('select[name="category"] > option')
```

This will find all the **option** elements within a particular **select** element, but only because they are direct children of the select box. For instance, this will not return any results:

```
> $('form > option')
```

Traversal

Selecting a set of elements from the DOM is an important step, but is only the first step in the process. Once a set of elements has been identified a common second step is to traverse from these elements to another set of elements.

A traversal function always starts with the results of a selection, and then performs a traversal operation on these elements to return a new set of elements.

A common traversal requirement is to traverse from an element, or set of elements, to their siblings. For instance, in tasks.html input fields and their labels are siblings because they share the same parent.

Sibling-based queries can be performed through the **siblings** function. If we want to find all siblings for the select box with the name of **category**, we can perform the following query:

```
> $('select[name="category"]').siblings()
```

If we want to limit the siblings to elements of type **label** we can add a selector to the **siblings** function:

```
> $('select[name="category"]').siblings('label')
```

Two other similar functions are **next** and **prev**. These return the next and previous sibling element of the selected element. For instance, the following returns the next sibling of all labels in the document:

```
> $('label').next()
```

while this returns the previous siblings of all the input fields in the document:

```
> $('input').prev()
```

Again, these functions also accept selection criteria if necessary.

Another common traversal requirement is to find specific parents of a given element or set of elements. For instance, we may wish to find the parent of all input fields. This can be achieved with the **parent** function:

```
> $('input').parent()
```

We may also wish to limit this to input fields that have **div** elements as their parents:

```
> $('input').parent('div')
```

A slight variant on this function is the **parents** function. Instead of returning immediate parents, this returns all ancestors that meet the selection criteria. For instance, the following returns the **section** element that is the ancestor of each input field:

```
> $('input').parents('section')
```

Yet another variant on the same theme is the **closest** function. This allows us to find the closest ancestor that matches a given selection criteria, starting with a specific set of nodes in the initial selection. This first examines the selected node against the criteria, then works its way up the DOM tree until it finds a match. For instance, if we want to find the closest **div** to each **label**, we could use the following selection:

```
> $('label').closest('div')
```

Another example of a traversal function is returning the **last** element. As we have seen, a pseudo-class on the selection itself also supports this. For instance, this returns the last row in the tasks table:

```
> $('#tblTasks tr').last()
```

As with all traversal functions, the **last** function also supports a parameter representing selection criteria, allowing you to find the last element that meets specific criteria.

The traversal functions we have examined up until this point all return a new set of elements that typically do not include any of the elements from the original selection. In some cases it is useful to retain the original selection while including additional elements found during the traversal. For instance, suppose we had returned a set of input fields, and now wish to also include all the labels in the result set. This can be achieved with the following:

```
> $('input').add('label')
```

A similar mechanism for achieving this is to augment any of the traversal functions above with a request to also add the original elements. For instance, the following call will return all labels and their closest div elements:

```
> $('label').closest('div').andSelf()
```

This particular line of code is a good time to introduce another important topic: chaining. Due to the fact that most jQuery function calls return an array of elements, and most jQuery function calls can be invoked on an array of elements, it is very easy to chain a set of function calls together, each acting on the elements returned by the call that preceded it. This process can continue almost indefinitely, for instance:

```
> $('input').parents('div').last().siblings().children()
```

If we trace this through, it is performing the following operation:

1. Find all **input** elements.

2. Find any **div** elements that are **parents** of these elements.

3. Limit the result set to the last **div** element.

4. Find its siblings.

5. Find their children.

Chaining allows for very concise code, but it also runs the risk of becoming dense and unreadable.

 This is similar to UNIX pipelining. Pipelining allows multiple applications to be chained together with the result of one forming the input of the other. In UNIX, the key design decision that allows this is the fact that applications return text on standard output, and accept text on standard input. In jQuery the key design decision that allows this is that functions can be called on arrays of elements, and these functions return arrays of elements.

Manipulation

The previous two sections on selection and traversal have shown you how a set of elements can be selected from the document. This section is going to introduce you to the ways you can manipulate documents once you have a set of elements to work with.

If you look at the tasks.html document you will see that the second row in the table has a class called **even** assigned to it. The basic idea is that every second row in the table will be given the **even** class, and this will change the background colour of the row to make the table easier to read.

As mentioned previously, a real world application would be better off performing this functionality with CSS, but performing this with jQuery provides a nice introduction to DOM manipulation.

Before beginning this section, remove the **even** class from the second row in the **table**. After this, refresh the tasks.html page in the browser and ensure all the rows have a white background.

In order to manipulate elements we must first select them. The selection criteria should be fairly standard by now. We first find all the **even** rows in the body of the **table** (this ensures we do not change the background of the header row):

```
> $('tbody tr:even')
```

This will actually return two rows, since jQuery is counting from 0 the first row in the table and the third row in the table are returned. This still suits our needs, since our only real concern is that every second row is shaded.

We can then manipulate these rows as following:

```
> $('tbody tr:even').addClass('even')
```

As soon as you execute this code you will see the DOM update, and the relevant rows of the table will be shaded with a new background color.

In addition to adding classes, we can also remove classes with **removeClass** and toggle classes with **toggleClass**. Toggling is a particularly useful technique since it removes the class if the element already has it, or adds the class if the element does not already have the class. This will be used in examples later in this book.

Another requirement we may wish to implement is to add a red * next to the label for all mandatory fields. We know how to find all the mandatory fields; they are the ones with a required attribute (regardless of the value assigned to this attribute):

```
> $('[required]')
```

and we can also find their labels as follows:

```
> $('[required="required"]').prev('label')
```

The file tasks.css also contains a class called **required** that is defined as follows:

```
.required {
    color: red;
}
```

In order to append the * to the **label**, we will include the * inside a **span**, and include that **span** within the **label**. This ensures it is separated from the label itself. We can dynamically append the **span** to the **label** as follows:

```
> $('[required="required"]').prev('label').append( '<span>*</span>')
```

If you execute this you will notice a * appear at the end of two of the labels on screen.

This is not quite the finished result, we still need to add the appropriate class to the new **span**s; so refresh the screen to remove these changes.

You may have noticed that the result of the call above was the labels that had been modified (rather than the **span**s that were appended to them). We therefore need to select the child **span**s to these elements, and add the **required** class to them:

```
> $('[required="required"]').prev('label').append(
'<span>*</span>').children('span').addClass('required')
```

Again, we have managed to achieve the entire operation in a single line through the use of chaining.

An important aspect to understand is that these changes have updated the Document Object Model in real time. In order to see this, highlight one of the red *, and choose "Inspect Element" from the right click menu (this is a shortcut to finding a specific element in the "Elements" tab of the developer tools). You will see the following:

```
▶ <div>…</div>
▼ <div>
  ▼ <label>
      "Required by"
      <span class="required">*</span>
    </label>
    <input type="date" required="required" name="requiredBy">
  </div>
```

Many of jQuery's manipulation functions can be utilized to insert new content either before or after existing content. **Append** is used to insert content inside a specific element, but other examples include:

• **after**: this adds content after each element, making the new content the next sibling of the original element. If we had used this in the example above, the **span** would occur after the closing **label** tag.

• **before**: this is similar to **after**, except the new element will appear before the original element. If we had used this in the example above, the **span** would have appeared immediately before the **label** element.

• **prepend**: this creates a new child element at the start of the element (as opposed to **append** which created the child at the end of the element). If we had used this in the example above, the * would have appeared to the left of the **label** text, but the **span** would still be a child of the **label**.

• **remove**: this completely removes an element from the document. You can use this to remove the newly added **span** elements.

• **replaceWith**: this replaces an element or set of elements with a new element or set of elements.

In the examples above we have been adding content to existing elements. Instead of adding content to elements, it is also possible to create content and add it to elements. For instance, the following is a valid jQuery call:

```
> $('<span>*</span>')
```

This returns the element specified by the HTML, although obviously that element is not part of the DOM at this point. It is then possible to call manipulation functions to add this element to the document:

```
> $('<span>*</span>').appendTo('label')
```

This will append a * as a child element to each **label** in the document. This approach can also used with the following functions:

• **insertBefore**: this function includes the new elements as siblings of the specified element or elements, but places them before them in the DOM.

• **insertAfter**: this function includes the new elements as siblings of the specified element or elements, but places them after them in the DOM.

• **prependTo**: this function includes the new elements as children of the specified element or elements, but places them at the start of the element, making them the first children.

The element inserted in this manner can be any HTML element or set of elements, including elements selected from the document.

In addition to adding new content to the DOM, some manipulation functions operate on characteristics of individual elements to either return information about them, or to manipulate this information. For instance, to find the value of the **select** element in the document we can execute:

```
> $('select').val()
```

The same function can be passed a value if we want to change the current value. If you execute the following the value of the **select** field will immediately change:

```
> $('select').val('Work')
```

An important note regarding this call is that if any event listeners are registered to detect changes to this element, they will not be notified with this call.

In order to notify any listeners of a change to the element, the following call could be used:

```
$('select').val('Work').change()
```

Event listeners will be covered in detail later in this chapter.

Other similar functions are:

• **html**: this returns or manipulates the html of an element.

• **text**: this returns the text (or content) of an element. The **text** is the content between the elements tags.

• **attr**: this returns or manipulates the value of an attribute on an element.

These functions are also a little different from some of the others we have examined in that they only operate on a single element. For instance, if you execute the following:

```
> $('div').html()
```

Only the HTML for the first element in the set of matched elements will be returned, rather than the HTML of all elements. Some jQuery functions are inherently limited in this way. In order to execute these functions on multiple elements, it is necessary to loop through those elements. This will be shown later in this chapter.

Events

The next aspect of jQuery to understand is events. When writing web applications, the application will need to respond to events initiated by the user.

These events may be any of the following:

• Clicking a link or button.

• Double clicking a button or link.

• Changing the value in a text field.

• Pressing a particular key inside an input field.

• Selecting an option in a select list.

• Focusing on an input field.

• Hovering the mouse over an element.

In addition to these user-initiated events, the application may wish to respond to browser-initiated events such as:

• The document has finished loading.

• The web browser window is resized.

• An error occurring.

This section will first explain the ways event listeners can be registered, and will then look at some of these events in detail.

Before beginning, we will add the examples above permanently to the tasks.html page. In order to do this, add the following block immediately before the closing </html> tag:

```
<script>
    $('[required="required"]').prev('label').append(
'<span>*</span>').children( 'span').addClass('required');

    $('tbody tr:even').addClass('even');
</script>
```

This is a block of inline JavaScript. We will eventually provide more structure to the web application, and remove code such as this from the HTML page, but for now this is a simple way of including JavaScript code in the web page.

We will now begin by adding a simple event to the sample web application we have been working on. We will start by defining the task creation section of the screen (inside the first **section** element), to be hidden when we first come into the screen.

We will also provide it an **id** so we can easily refer to it:

```
<section id="taskCreation" class="not">
```

The **not** class is defined in tasks.css, and provides a simple mechanism for hiding an element. It is defined as follows:

```
.not {
  display:none;
}
```

Next, we will modify the link with the text "Add Task" to have an **id**. This will allow us to select it more conveniently with jQuery:

```
<a href="#" id="btnAddTask">Add task</a>
```

Finally, we will add the following code to the script section of tasks.html:

```
$('#btnAddTask').click(function(evt) {
  evt.preventDefault();
  $('#taskCreation').removeClass('not');
});
```

This code will be explained in detail below.

The entire page should now look like this (changes are highlighted in bold):

```
<!DOCTYPE html>
<html lang="en">
<head>
<meta charset="utf-8">
<title>Task list</title>
<link rel="stylesheet" type="text/css" href="styles/tasks.css"
    media="screen" />
<script src="scripts/jquery-2.0.3.js"></script>
</head>
<body>
    <header>
        <span>Task list</span>
    </header>
    <main>
        <section id="taskCreation" class="not">
<form>
```

```
        <div>
            <label>Task</label> <input type="text"
required="required"
                name="task" class="large"
placeholder="Breakfast at Tiffanys" />
        </div>
        <div>
            <label>Required by</label> <input type="date"
required="required"
                name="requiredBy" />
        </div>
        <div>
            <label>Category</label> <select name="category">
                <option value="Personal">Personal</option>
                <option value="Work">Work</option>
            </select>
        </div>
        <nav>
            <a href="#">Save task</a> <a href="#">Clear
task</a>
        </nav>
    </form>
</section>
<section>
    <table id="tblTasks">
        <colgroup>
            <col width="50%">
            <col width="25%">
            <col width="25%">
        </colgroup>
        <thead>
            <tr>
                <th>Name</th>
                <th>Due</th>
                <th>Category</th>
```

```
                </tr>
            </thead>
            <tbody>
                <tr>
                    <td>Return library books</td>
                    <td><time datetime="2013-10-14">2013-10-
14</time></td>
                    <td>Personal</td>
                </tr>
                <tr>
                    <td>Perform project demo to stakeholders</td>
                    <td><time datetime="2013-10-14">2013-10-
14</time></td>
                    <td>Work</td>
                </tr>
                <tr>
                    <td>Meet friends for dinner</td>
                    <td><time datetime="2013-10-14">2013-10-
14</time></td>
                    <td>Personal</td>
                </tr>
            </tbody>
        </table>
        <nav>
            <a href="#" id="btnAddTask">Add task</a>
        </nav>
    </section>
  </main>
  <footer>You have 3 tasks</footer>
</body>
<script>
    $('[required="required"]').prev('label').append(
'<span>*</span>').children( 'span').addClass('required');
    $('tbody tr:even').addClass('even');
```

```
$('#btnAddTask').click(function(evt) {
    evt.preventDefault();
    $('#taskCreation').removeClass('not');
});
</script>
</html>
```

If you reload the page, you should see that the task creation section (with all the input fields) is not displayed when the page initially loads. If you click the "Add task" button however, this section will immediately appear.

If you look at the event handler code you will see some familiar features. First, we select the element we wish to add an event listener to using standard jQuery selection criteria:

```
> $('#btnAddTask')
```

Next we call the appropriate jQuery function on this element to add a click listener; this function is called **click** and it accepts a JavaScript function as its parameter. In this example, the JavaScript function passed to the click function is created on the fly as an anonymous function. This could also have been written as follows:

```
function btnAddClicked(evt) {
    $(evt.target).preventDefault();
    $('#taskCreation').removeClass('not');
}


$('#btnAddTask').click(btnAddClicked);
```

The technical term for the function we have passed to the **click** function is a callback. This is because the function is not executed immediately; it is executed when a specific event occurs (the user clicks the button). jQuery, like many other JavaScript libraries, makes extensive uses of callbacks, and we will see many other examples in the sections below.

You will also see that our function accepts a parameter called **evt**. When jQuery invokes the function we passed to it, it will provide an object as a parameter representing the event that has occurred.

The most useful feature that can be obtained from the event object is the element that caused the event. The same event listener may be added to many elements, therefore we will often need to find out which of these elements had the event invoked on it. This can be extracted from the event object as follows:

```
evt.target
```

It may not be immediately obvious, but the object returned as the target is a plain DOM object rather than a jQuery wrapped DOM object. This may sound like a minor point, but it means that it is not possible to invoke jQuery functions on this element. For instance, if we attempt to call the **html** function on this element, the following error will occur:

```
> evt.target.html()
⊃ ▶ TypeError: Object [object HTMLAnchorElement] has no method 'html'
> |
```

Whenever you are presented with a native DOM object, it is easy to convert it to jQuery wrapped object by selecting it:

```
$(evt.target)
```

The result of this will expose all the standard jQuery functionality:

```
> $(evt.target).html()
  "Add task"
```

You will also notice the following line in the click handler:

```
evt.preventDefault();
```

A single element can have multiple event listeners attached to it. Some of these will be added explicitly by the application, but the browser may add its own action implicitly. These implicit event listeners are called the default action of the element; for instance, a hyperlink has a default action that invokes its specified URL when it is clicked.

In this web application we do not want hyperlinks to exhibit this default behavior, otherwise the page would be refreshed every time the user clicked a button. Therefore we call **preventDefault** on the event to signal that the element's default action should be suppressed.

Using hyperlinks instead of button elements is a personal preference. Many designers have historically preferred them, since they tend to be easier to style, and more flexible to use. There is however a strong argument in favor of using button elements in these cases.

The final aspect of this event handler is the removal of the class that was causing this element to be hidden, which should be familiar code by now:

```
$('#taskCreation').removeClass('not');
```

It is possible to add click listeners to any HTML element. For instance, we can add a feature to the **table** so that when the user clicks a row it will highlight in bold. If they then click the row again it will return to normal.

The tasks.css file already contains a class that can set the text of an element to bold:

```
.rowHighlight {
    font-weight:bold;
}
```

As a first attempt at this code, we will try adding the following to the script block of tasks.html:

```
$('tbody tr').click(function(evt) {
```

```
    $(evt.target).toggleClass('rowHighlight');
});
```

This is adding a click listener to all rows in the **table** body. When invoked, this will add the **rowHighlighted** class to the element that was clicked.

If you debug this you will notice that the value of **evt.target** is in fact the element that has been clicked on (the **td** element) rather than the **tr** element, therefore only a single cell highlights in bold.

 The next chapter will address debugging JavaScript code. If you are unfamiliar with the Chrome debugger, and would like to see this for yourself, you may want to jump ahead to that chapter.

As a second attempt, we could try to find the **tr** element that is the parent of the element that was clicked, and add the class to this element. This also will not work, since **td** elements have been defined with normal font-styles in tasks.css, therefore they will not inherit font-style from their parents.

What we want to do is add this class to all the **td** elements in the row that is selected. We could attempt this as follows:

```
$('tbody tr').click(function(evt) {
    $(evt.target).siblings().toggleClass('rowHighlight');
});
```

There are two problems remaining with this. The **siblings** function returns a set of all the siblings, but leaves out the element that has been clicked, so all cells except the one clicked will highlight. Ee can solve this with the following:

```
$('tbody tr').click(function(evt) {
    $(evt.target).siblings().andSelf( ).toggleClass( 'rowHighlight');
});
```

The next problem is the **td** element that contains the **time** element. If the **time** element is clicked, the list of siblings will be empty, since the **time** element does not have any siblings. Before finding the siblings we therefore need to first find the closest **td** element to the one clicked.

As mentioned earlier, the **closest** function begins by examining the selected element, and only ascends the tree if that does not match the requirements. Therefore, the closest **td** to a **td** is itself, but the closest **td** to a **time** element is its parent.

The following code therefore meets our requirements:

```
$('tbody tr').click(function(evt) {
    $(evt.target).closest( 'td').siblings().andSelf( ).toggleClass(
'rowHighlight');
});
```

Finally, note that we are using the **toggleClass** function. Rather than checking whether the elements have the class **rowHighlight**, and adding it if they don't, and removing it if they do, we can let jQuery do the work for us.

In the examples above we are adding event listeners to elements in the document when the page is loaded. A complication with event listeners is that we might want to add them to elements that are not in the document yet. Due to the fact we can dynamically add elements to the DOM, we may want event listeners automatically added to these elements when they meet specified selection criteria.

If we consider the case of the event listener that highlights selected rows in the table, we may want this to work even if rows are dynamically added to the table after the page has loaded.

Fortunately jQuery has an elegant solution to this problem using the **on** function. The first part of the solution involves specifying the portion of the document that will contain any new elements, in our case that may be:

```
$('#tblTasks tbody')
```

We could alternatively say we want to add the event listener to any new elements anywhere in the document with:

```
$(document)
```

Next we specify the type of event listener we want to attach, the type of element we want the event listener added against, and the callback we want executed.

In order to demonstrate this, we will add a click listener to be able to delete each row in the table.

Before beginning, we need to add navigation buttons to each row in the table body. Add the following to each row in the **tbody** immediately before the </tr> (there are 3 of them):

```
<td>
  <nav>
    <a href="#" class="editRow">Edit</a>
    <a href="#" class="completeRow">Complete</a>
    <a href="#" class="deleteRow" >Delete</a>
  </nav>
</td>
```

In addition, add a new header cell inside the table header immediately before the </tr>:

```
<th>Actions</th>
```

Finally, to make sure the columns are sized correctly, change the column groups for the table as follows:

```
<colgroup>
    <col width="40%">
    <col width="15%">
    <col width="15%">
```

```
    <col width="30%">
</colgroup>
```

In order to verify the changes, executing the following should return three elements:

```
$('.deleteRow')
```

We can now add an event listener as follows:

```
$('#tblTasks tbody').on('click', '.deleteRow',    function(evt) {
    evt.preventDefault();
    $(evt.target).parents('tr').remove();
});
```

When an element with the class **deleteRow** is clicked, this event listener will find the **tr** element that is a parent of this element:

```
$(evt.target).parents('tr')
```

It will then remove this element from the document using the **remove** function.

Naturally this works for the three rows that were in the table when the page loaded. If you want to prove that this approach works for rows added directly to the DOM, you can add a new row to the table with the following code:

```
$('#tblTasks tbody tr:first' ).clone().insertAfter('#tblTasks tbody
tr:last')
```

This code will select the first row from the table, clone it, to create a new row, and then insert it after the last row in the table. You will be able to then delete this row from the table using its delete button, without having to add an event listener explicitly to the button.

 Earlier versions of jQuery used a function called **live** to add dynamic event listeners. This function has been deprecated and should not be used.

So far we have concentrated on click events. There are many other events that can be listened for with jQuery. The following are the other common events, all of which work in the same basic way:

- **dblclick**: is invoked when an element is clicked twice in quick succession.

- **hover**: is invoked when the mouse hovers over the element.

- **mousedown**: is invoked when the mouse button is pressed, and before the button is release.

- **mouseup**: is invoked when the mouse button is released.

- **keypress**: is invoked each time the user types a key into an element, such as a text field.

- **keydown**: is invoked when the user presses a key, but before the output is reflected on screen. This allows you to veto the action with preventDefault.

- **blur**: is invoked when the focus leaves a form field. This is useful when you wish to validate content after the user has finished typing.

• **change**: is invoked when the value of a form field changes.

• **focus**: is invoked when the form field receives focus.

For a complete list of events, see the jQuery documentation.

Before finishing this section, we will make a minor change to ensure that our event handlers are not added before the DOM has been fully constructed. Ideally we want to start processing scripts after the DOM has been constructed, even if all resources (such as images) have not been loaded. Due to the way JavaScript works, it is possible that it will begin processing before the DOM has loaded, in which case elements will not be available when selected:

 Technically in our case we do not need to worry about this, since our script is declared at the bottom of the page. It is however a good habit to use the approach suggested below, even in this case.

In order to detect that the DOM has fully loaded we can listen for the **ready** event:

```
$(document).ready()
```

As with all event listeners, this accepts a callback function, therefore we will change the code as follows:

```
$(document).ready(function() {
    $('[required="required"]').prev('label').append(
'<span>*</span>').children( 'span').addClass('required');

    $('tbody tr:even').addClass('even');


    $('#btnAddTask').click(function(evt) {
        evt.preventDefault();
        $('#taskCreation').removeClass('not');
    });


    $('tbody tr').click(function(evt) {
        $(evt.target).closest('td').siblings().
            andSelf().toggleClass('rowHighlight');
    });


    $('#tblTasks tbody').on('click', '.deleteRow', function(evt) {
        evt.preventDefault();
        $(evt.target).parents('tr').remove();
    });
```

```
});
```

If you need to delay code execution until all resources have loaded, the **load** event can be used instead:

```
$(document).load()
```

Writing jQuery Plugins

One of the reasons jQuery has become so popular is that it is trivial to write plugins that integrate with jQuery. This has led to a huge number of plugins freely available under the MIT license, and also allows you to write your own custom plugins.

A jQuery plugin usually works by performing an operation on an element, or set of elements returned from a jQuery selection. Just like standard jQuery functions, depending on how the plugin is written, it may be capable of acting on a whole set of elements, or just a single element.

In this section we are going to write a plugin that can be executed on a **form** element that has been selected using jQuery. This plugin will then return an object where the property names on the object are the form field names, and the values are the values of that field. Effectively this plugin is going to serialize the values on a form into an object. We will also allow this plugin to operate in the opposite direction: to de-serialize an object onto a **form**.

This plugin will take advantage of programming by convention. We will assume that the object names and the form field names should always match, even though there will be nothing in the code that insists on this.

Programming by convention does have disadvantages. For instance, if anyone changed the name of a field this will result in changes to the property on the objects serialized from that form, and that may in turn break other code that had expectations about what those properties would be. Programming by convention can significantly reduce the amount of code required to implement functionality however.

Plugins work in jQuery by passing the jQuery function to the plugin function, which will then extend the jQuery function by creating an object with a set of new functions in it.

It is not particularly important that you understand this process, but the boilerplate code for adding new functions to jQuery looks like this:

```
(function($) {
    $.fn.extend({
        action: function() {}
    });
})(jQuery);
```

In this case we are adding a single new jQuery function called **action**. This could then be invoked as follows:

```
> $('div').action()
```

Inside the function we can use the **this** variable to access the element or elements that the function has been executed on, for instance in the example above, all the div elements. This will either represent an array of jQuery elements, or a single jQuery element. In our example we are always going to assume that **this** is a single element.

To begin, we will write a rudimentary version of the serialize function that simply writes the contents of the **form** to the console log:

```
(function($) {
  $.fn.extend({
    toObject: function() {
      console.log(this.serialize());
    }
  });
})(jQuery);
```

This implementation adds a new function to jQuery called **toObject**, and is going to take advantage of a function already available in jQuery that serializes a form into a string.

Add this to the script section of the web page, refresh the web page, and click "Add task". Enter values into all the fields, and then call the following from the console:

```
> $('form').toObject()
```

This should print out a text string with the contents of the form.

Now that we have a basic implementation, we can start writing the code needed to return an object with properties populated from the form.

Although jQuery does not have a function for serializing a form into an object, it does have a function for serializing a form to an array. This function returns an array where each form field is represented by an element in the array, and consists of a name and a value. In order to see this function in action, execute the following:

```
> $('form').serializeArray()
```

We will use this as the basis of our implementation, and iterate over the array using a jQuery helper function called **each**:

```
$.each($('form').serializeArray(), function(i, v) {

});
```

jQuery has a number of utility functions available with "$." prefixes. Unlike other jQuery functions, these are not used for selecting elements, and they cannot be invoked on a set of elements.

This particular function will iterate over an array and pass each index and value to the callback function we provide. To see this in action, try executing the following:

```
> $.each([1,4,8,16,32], function(i, v) {
    console.log('index: '+i);
```

```
        console.log('value: '+v)
});
```

This should print out:

```
index: 0
value: 1
index: 1
value: 4
index: 2
value: 8
index: 3
value: 16
index: 4
value: 32
```

Unlike the standard JavaScript **for** and **while** loops, the **$.each** helper has the ability to iterate over both arrays and objects.

Now that the skeleton of **toObject** is in place, we can complete the implementation as follows:

```
(function($) {
  $.fn.extend({
    toObject: function() {
      var result = {}
      $.each(this.serializeArray(), function(i, v) {
        result[v.name] = v.value;
      });
      return result;
    }
  });
})(jQuery);
```

If you now execute the following:

```
> o = $('form').toObject()
```

The variable o will contain an object, with properties reflecting the names of the field in the form. It is therefore possible to execute the following:

```
> o.task
```

You will notice that the implementation starts by creating an empty object. Properties are then added to the object for each form element. The implementation uses the [] bracket approach to add properties, rather than the "." notation. This is important, because the name of fields may not conform to the standards required by JavaScript when using the "." notation.

Now that we have a **toObject** function, we can add a second function to de-serialize an object back onto a form. In order to add a second function, we simply create a new property in the object we are creating to extend jQuery. This function will be called **fromObject** and accepts an object as a parameter:

```
(function($) {
  $.fn.extend({
    toObject: function() {
      var result = {}
      $.each(this.serializeArray(), function(i, v) {
        result[v.name] = v.value;
      });
      return result;
    },
    fromObject: function(obj) {


    }
  });
})(jQuery);
```

The first task of this function will be to extract all the form fields from the **form** this function is called on (which again, will be represented by the **this** variable). We can extract the input fields with the following:

```
this.find('input')
```

The only problem is that this will not include select boxes, since they are not considered types of input fields. Fortunately, jQuery provides a selector that does return all input fields, including select fields:

```
this.find(':input')
```

Once all the form fields are found, the implementation will iterate over all the fields and extract their name attribute. It will then look in the object for a property with that name, and if there is one, it we will set the value of the field from the value of the property:

```
fromObject: function(obj) {
  $.each(this.find(':input'), function(i,v) {
    var name = $(v).attr('name');
    if (obj[name]) {
      $(v).val(obj[name]);
    } else {
```

```
    $(v).val('');
    }
  });
}
```

You will notice that we add the **$()** construct around the references to **v**. This is because the value returned is a native DOM object; therefore it is necessary to convert it to a jQuery object in order to use the **attr** method.

With that implementation in place you should be able to change values in the form, and then call the following to repopulate it back to the original values stored in the **o** variable:

```
> $('form').fromObject(o)
```

The final version of the jQuery plugin is as follows:

```
(function($) {
  $.fn.extend({
    toObject: function() {
      var result = {}
      $.each(this.serializeArray(), function(i, v) {
        result[v.name] = v.value;
      });
      return result;
    },
    fromObject: function(obj) {
      $.each(this.find(':input'), function(i,v) {
        var name = $(v).attr('name');
        if (obj[name]) {
          $(v).val(obj[name]);
        } else {
          $(v).val('');
        }
      });
    }
  });
})(jQuery);
```

Using existing plugins

Before writing your own plugin, it is useful to check if any plugins are already available that meet your needs. There is a vast library of plugins available on the Internet. Some are well supported and widely used; others are unsupported, or used by a handful of people.

Most plugins are available under the MIT license, meaning you are free to modify them in any way you need.

In this section we are going to use a plugin for generating HTML from a template. The plugin we will use is jQuery Template, and is available here:

https://github.com/BorisMoore/jquery-tmpl

You can choose to download either jquery.tmpl.js or jquery.tmpl.min.js.

Alternatively, you can use the following CDN version:

http://ajax.aspnetcdn.com/ajax/jquery.templates/beta1/jquery.tmpl.js

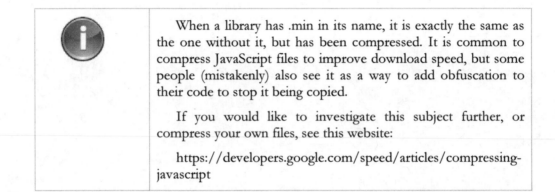

When a library has .min in its name, it is exactly the same as the one without it, but has been compressed. It is common to compress JavaScript files to improve download speed, but some people (mistakenly) also see it as a way to add obfuscation to their code to stop it being copied.

If you would like to investigate this subject further, or compress your own files, see this website:

https://developers.google.com/speed/articles/compressing-javascript

This plugin was originally intended to form part of the core jQuery library, but these plans have not come to fruition. The library is now largely unsupported, but is still a useful templating library (I still use it extensively), and will be used here primarily to demonstrate the use of a jQuery plugin.

If you would like to use a supported templating library on a project, I recommend the Underscore library, which provides templating functionality that performs essentially the same role.

In order to use a downloaded version of jQuery Template, first copy it to the scripts folder of the project. Once in place, add the following to the head section of the page, but **after** the main jQuery import:

```
<head>
<meta charset="utf-8">
<title>Task list</title>
<link rel="stylesheet" type="text/css" href="styles/tasks.css"
media="screen" />
<script
src="http://ajax.googleapis.com/ajax/libs/jquery/2.0.3/jquery.min.js"><
/script>
<script src="scripts/jquery-tmpl.js"></script>
```

```
</head>
```

 You may notice that it is no longer necessary to specify that the language of a script file is "text/javascript". HTML5 assumes by default that scripts are JavaScript.

This is all that is required in order to start using the jQuery Template plugin. When the script loads it will automatically add new features to jQuery, just as our own custom plugin added new features to jQuery.

When new tasks are created via the form, we need to dynamically add them to the **table**; this means creating a new **tr** element in the table, and adding the appropriate **td** columns.

We could achieve this with jQuery directly by generating a string to represent the HTML and then appending it to the table. As we saw earlier in this chapter, it is possible to generate elements directly out of HTML and add them into the DOM.

Constructing HTML within code is error prone however, and it will be more convenient if we can write the basic structure of the row as HTML, and leave placeholders for the dynamic content.

 Templating libraries are widely used in software development. Like jQuery template, they provide basic control structures such as loops and branching, and allow placeholders for parameters.

jQuery template allows us to define the following template in the HTML page:

```
<script id="taskRow" type="text/x-jQuery-tmpl">
<tr>
  <td>${task}</td>
  <td><time datetime="${requiredBy}"> ${requiredBy}</time></td>
  <td>${category}</td>
  <td>
    <nav>
      <a href="#">Edit</a>
      <a href="#">Complete</a>
      <a href="#" class="deleteRow">Delete</a>
    </nav>
  </td>
</tr>
</script>
```

This can be added at the very bottom of the page, before the </html> (not inside the other **script** block). Note that this is essentially just a block of HTML, except it contains placeholders for values. The placeholders are inside the following constructs: **${}**.

Also note that this is not a standard JavaScript block, since it is defined as type **text/x-jQuery-tmpl**. The block also contains an ID, which is not typically needed in standard script blocks.

We now are going to implement a rudimentary version of the save functionality. Start by adding an ID to the save button:

```
<a href="#" id="saveTask">Save task</a>
```

Next, add a **click** event listener to the save task button. This is going to convert the form data into an object using the plugin we developed in the last section. It is then going to pass this object to the template we constructed above. Notice that in the template the placeholder names match the property names that will appear on our task object.

The template will generate a block of HTML, which we will then append to the table body. Add the following code to the **script** section of tasks.html alongside the other event handlers:

```
$('#saveTask').click(function(evt) {

  evt.preventDefault();

  var task = $('form').toObject();

  $('#taskRow').tmpl(task).appendTo($('#tblTasks tbody'));

});
```

As you can see, two lines of code are sufficient to convert the form to an object, and include the contents in the **table**, and this could be condensed to one line with relative ease.

As stated above, this is a rudimentary version of the save functionality. For instance, it does not contain any validation; therefore you can add invalid data to the table. The tasks also disappear if we refresh the page. This, and other minor issues, will be fixed once we start to turn this into a true web application in a couple of chapters time.

Now that the save is implemented we can remove the three rows that were added to the table by default each time the page was loaded, and add rows using the "Add task" and "Save task" functionality. In addition, the rows added should be able to be deleted using the "Delete task" option.

The tasks.html page should now contain the following markup:

```
<!DOCTYPE html>

<html lang="en">

<head>

<meta charset="utf-8">

<title>Task list</title>

<link rel="stylesheet" type="text/css" href="styles/tasks.css"
    media="screen" />

<script src="scripts/jquery-2.0.3.js"></script>

<script src="scripts/jquery-tmpl.js"></script>

</head>
```

```
<body>
  <header>
    <span>Task list</span>
  </header>
  <main>
    <section id="taskCreation" class="not">
      <form>
        <div>
          <label>Task</label>
          <input type="text" required="required"
                 name="task" class="large"
                 placeholder="Breakfast at Tiffanys" />
        </div>
        <div>
          <label>Required by</label>
          <input type="date" required="required"
                 name="requiredBy" />
        </div>
        <div>
          <label>Category</label>
          <select name="category">
            <option value="Personal">Personal</option>
            <option value="Work">Work</option>
          </select>
        </div>
        <nav>
          <a href="#" id="saveTask">Save task</a>
          <a href="#">Clear task</a>
        </nav>
      </form>
    </section>
    <section>
      <table id="tblTasks">
        <colgroup>
```

```
                <col width="40%">
                <col width="15%">
                <col width="15%">
                <col width="30%">
            </colgroup>
            <thead>
            <tr>
                <th>Name</th>
                <th>Due</th>
                <th>Category</th>
                <th>Actions</th>
            </tr>
            </thead>
            <tbody>
            </tbody>
        </table>
        <nav>
            <a href="#" id="btnAddTask">Add task</a>
        </nav>
    </section>
    </main>
    <footer>You have 3 tasks</footer>
</body>
<script>
$(document).ready(function() {
    $('[required="required"]').prev('label').
        append( '<span>*</span>').children( 'span').
        addClass('required');
    $('tbody tr:even').addClass('even');
    $('#btnAddTask').click(function(evt) {
        evt.preventDefault();
        $('#taskCreation').removeClass('not');
    });
    $('tbody tr').click(function(evt) {
```

```
        $(evt.target).closest('td' ).siblings().
            andSelf().toggleClass('rowHighlight');
    });

    $('#tblTasks tbody').on('click', '.deleteRow', function(evt) {
        evt.preventDefault();
        $(evt.target).parents('tr').remove();
    });

    $('#saveTask').click(function(evt) {
        evt.preventDefault();
        var task = $('form').toObject();
        $('#taskRow').tmpl(task).appendTo($('#tblTasks tbody'));
    });
});

(function($) {
  $.fn.extend({
    toObject: function() {
      var result = {}
      $.each(this.serializeArray(), function(i, v) {
        result[v.name] = v.value;
      });
      return result;
    },
    fromObject: function(obj) {
        $.each(this.find(':input'), function(i,v) {
          var name = $(v).attr('name');
          if (obj[name]) {
            $(v).val(obj[name]);
          } else {
            $(v).val('');
          }
        });
```

```
        }
    });
})(jQuery);

</script>

<script id="taskRow" type="text/x-jQuery-tmpl">
<tr>
    <td>${task}</td>
    <td><time datetime="${requiredBy}"> ${requiredBy}</time></td>
    <td>${category}</td>
    <td>
        <nav>
            <a href="#">Edit</a>
            <a href="#">Complete</a>
            <a href="#" class="deleteRow">Delete</a>
        </nav>
    </td>
</tr>
</script>

</html>
```

Conclusion

This chapter has introduced all the important aspects of jQuery that deal with DOM manipulation. As has been demonstrated, jQuery provides an elegant and concise set of function calls for selecting, traversing and manipulating the DOM, along with adding event listeners.

Although jQuery does not do anything that could not be done natively with the DOM API (or other libraries such as Dojo for that matter), jQuery provides the following benefits:

• It takes care of any quirks that may exist in different versions of web browsers.

• It uses the same basic set of selectors as CSS, meaning anyone who understands CSS can quickly adapt to jQuery.

• It provides a concise and intuitive set of function calls that are easy to learn, and easy to use in conjunction with one another.

• It is easy to extend jQuery to solve new problems.

• jQuery is widely used, therefore there is a wealth of information and help available online.

There are several aspects of jQuery that have not been examined as yet. Foremost amongst these is the AJAX API which will be introduced later in this book. Several other jQuery topics will also be introduced at the appropriate point in the book.

7 DEBUGGING

Now that we have some working code, it is worth taking a step back to look at the development tools that can help when writing JavaScript based web applications.

Probably the most important tool for development purposes is a debugger. Debuggers allow a software engineer to examine an application while it is running, and therefore analyse the cause of any problems.

In order to start the debugger, first open the tasks.html page in Chrome. Then use one of the following approaches to open the development tools:

- Command+Option+i on OSX

- F12 or Ctrl+Shift+I on Windows

Once the familiar console is open, click on the sources tab:

If you scroll to the bottom of the tasks.html page you will see the JavaScript that has been added in the previous chapter.

Find the following piece of code in the file:

```
$('#btnAddTask').click(function(evt) {
```

```
    evt.preventDefault();

    $('#taskCreation').removeClass('not');

});
```

And click in the left hand margin on the line evt.preventDefault();. The line should highlight in blue; you will see this on line 88 in the screenshot below (the line in your version may differ):

```
79          </menu>
80      </section>
81
82      <footer>You have 3 tasks</footer>
83  </body>
84  <script>
85
86  $(document).ready(function() {
87      $('#btnAddTask').click(function(evt) {
88          evt.preventDefault();
89          $('#taskCreation').removeClass('not');
90      });
91
92      $('tbody tr').click(function(evt) {
93          $(evt.target).closest('td').siblings().andSelf().toggleClass('rowHighlight');
94      });
95
96      $('#tblTasks tbody').on('click', '.deleteRow', function(evt) {
97          $(evt.target).parents('tr').remove();
98      });
```

This is a breakpoint, which indicates that the debugger should stop execution when it reaches this line.

Now, keeping the development tools open, click the "Add Task" button on the main web page. When you click this, Chrome will stop execution at the breakpoint.

Now that the debugger has stopped at a breakpoint we have several choices.

As a first step, we can interact with the JavaScript environment, including any local variables that are in scope. You can see on the right hand side that Chrome is telling us there are two local variables in scope:

▼ Scope Variables

▼ Local
  ▶ evt: jQuery.Event
  ▶ this: a#btnAddTask

In order to interact with these, click on the Console tab and type:

```
> evt
```

This will display the event object, which can be opened up to show its properties:

In addition, we can execute our own code here if we would like to try something out. Any code we type will use the local variables currently in scope. For instance, we can execute the following code to get the **id** of the element that has been clicked:

```
> $(evt.target).attr("id")
```

We can even change objects in scope, for instance, we could add a new attribute to the element:

```
> $(evt.target).attr("data-test", "test")
```

This provides an excellent environment in which to write snippets of code, because you receive immediate feedback from the browser on each line of code you write.

We can also examine the current call stack. This is the list of calls that have led to this line of code being called:

▼ Call Stack

(anonymous function)

jQuery.event.dispatch

elemData.handle

You can then click on any of the function calls in the stack, and Chrome will take you to that line of code. Once you are taken to that line of code you will have access to the environment that line has access to it, including all local variables (which may be different from the variables that were available on the line where the breakpoint was hit).

In addition to interacting with the JavaScript environment, the other main purpose of the debugger is to step through code. This allows you to watch the program execute line by line in real-time, and makes it easier to understand any issues or defects that may be encountered.

Stepping through code can be achieved with these controls:

You can hover over each button to see its purpose:

• "Resume script execution" will cause execution to start again.

• "Step over next function call" will step to the line immediately below the one currently stopped on.

• "Step into the next function call" will cause the debugger to enter any function calls on the current line in the order that they will be executed.

• "Step out of current function" is useful when you have stepped into a function, but would now like to return to the point where the code entered the function call.

In cases where your code is split between several files, you can click the "Show navigator" button in the top right of the debugger and choose the file that contains code you want to add break points to:

```
   Elements    Resources    Network    Sources

 Sources  Content scripts    □ |||

 ▼ ○ file://                          >
   ▼ □ Users/aileetan/workspace/t
     ▼ □ scripts
         ☑ jquery-2.0.3.js          id="btnAddTask"
     ▶ □ styles
       ☑ tasks.html                 asks</footer>


                                     on() {
                                     .ck(function(evt
                                     lt();
                                     ').removeClass(
```

Another very useful feature of the debugger is the pause button at the bottom of the menu:

```
 □   >≣   Q   ⓿   { }   Line 1, Column 1
```

If you click this once it will turn blue. This will cause the debugger to automatically pause on any exception – including handled exceptions.

If you click it once more it will turn purple. This will cause the debugger to automatically pause on all unhandled exceptions. This is very useful, since it is not always obvious that a JavaScript error has occurred. As long as this setting is in place, and you always run the application with the development tools open, you will not miss any errors, and will be able to debug them while they are occurring.

In order to see this in action, remove the existing breakpoint, and change the code:

```
$('#btnAddTask').click(function(evt) {

    evt.preventDefault();

  $('#taskCreation').removeClass('not');

});
```

to

```
$('#btnAddTask').click(function(evt) {

    evt.callUnknownFunction();

    $('#taskCreation').removeClass('not');

});
```

Since JavaScript is not a type checked language, it is not until run-time that an exception will be caused by this change. If you now refresh the screen and click the "Add task" button you will see that the debugger automatically stops on this line:

```
  Elements    Resources    Network    Sources    Timeline    Profiles    Audits    Console

 tasks.html ×  jquery.min.js
73                        </td>
74                    </tr>
75                </tbody>
76            </table>
77            <menu>
78                <a href="#" id="btnAddTask">Add task</a>
79            </menu>
80        </section>
81
82        <footer>You have 3 tasks</footer>
83  </body>
84  <script>
85
86  $(document).ready(function() {
87      $('#btnAddTask').click(function(evt) {
            evt.callUnknownFunction();
89          $('#taskCreation').removeClass('not');
90      });
91
92      $('tbody tr').click(function(evt) {
93          $(evt.target).closest('td').siblings().andSelf().toggleClass('rowHighlight');
94      });

 ⌨  ≥Ξ  Q  ⓪  { }  Line 1, Column 1
```

You can now interact with the environment in the console. For instance, you can execute this line of code to see what is wrong with it:

```
> evt.callUnknownFunction();
```

```
TypeError: Object #<Object> has no method 'callUnknownFunction'
```

Finally, you can use the button in the bottom left of the debugger to undock the debugger into a separate window. This is very useful if you have dual screens, since the debugger can run in one window, and the browser in the other.

Before finishing, remember to change your add task event listener back to the correct implementation.

8 MOVING TO A WEB SERVER

Up until this point we have been loading the tasks.html page directly from the file-system. We now need to move to serving our pages from a web server. Several of the APIs we will be using in the next few chapters rely on pages being served from a specific domain – even if that domain is "localhost" rather than "yourserver.com".

For instance, if a website wants to store data on the client, the browser must be able to distinguish between the data created by one website and the data created by another. Rules such as this are referred to as "same-origin policies". The browser uses the domain name and the port (which usually defaults to 80 or 443 – but will be 8080 in our case) to determine the origin of a web page, and restricts interaction between pages with different origins (except where specified).

This chapter will help get you started with the Mongoose webserver. This is one of the smallest web servers available, and requires very minimal configuration.

OSX

Download the OSX installer from:

http://cesanta.com/downloads.html

Once this has downloaded, perform the following steps:

1. Double click on the DMG file and drag it to applications.

2. Open the finder, and go to the "Applications" folder.

3. Double click on Mongoose.

The Mongoose application can now be configured via the icon in the taskbar at the top of the screen:

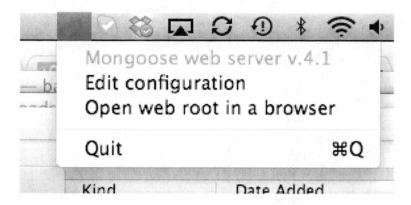

Click on "Edit configuration". This will open in a text editor. Locate the following line:

```
# document_root /Applications/Mongoose.app/Contents/MacOS
```

Change the directory to be directory that contains the tasks.html file. In addition, remove the # at the start of the line, e.g.

```
document_root /html5/tasks
```

Quit the Mongoose web server using this menu and restart it (by double clicking on the application in the "Applications" folder).

Open Chrome, and enter:

http://localhost:8080/tasks.html

This should show the main tasks web page.

Windows

Download the Windows Executable (no install required) installer from:

http://cesanta.com/downloads.html

Once this downloads, perform the following steps:

1. Copy the exe file to the same directory that contains tasks.html.

2. Double click on the executable to start Mongoose.

The Mongoose application can now be configured via the icon in the taskbar at the bottom of the screen (although no configuration is required in this case):

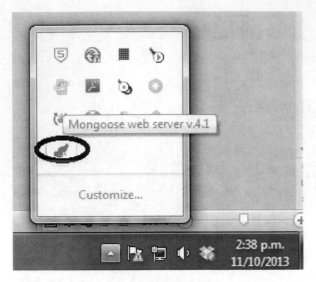

Open Chrome, and enter:

http://localhost:8080/tasks.html

This should show the main tasks web page.

9 BUILDING THE WEB APPLICATION

You have now learned the basic technology required to create the sample web application. Although we have some working code on the existing web page, it is not structured in a manner that would allow it to scale to become a large web application.

In the first section of this chapter are going to refactor the code that we have created into a structure that follows a more rigorous design. This will then allow us to add additional functionality to the web application.

As a first step, we will extract the jQuery plugin that we wrote to serialize and de-serialize objects into forms, and place this in a file called jquery-serialization.js in the scripts folder.

We will also want to move most of the JavaScript code from tasks.html into a JavaScript file called tasks-controller.js. To start with, we will just create an empty file called tasks-controller.js in the scripts folder.

We will then import these 2 script files in the head section of the HTML page. (Ensure that these are added after the jQuery import).

```
<script src="scripts/jquery-serialization.js"></script>
<script src="scripts/tasks-controller.js"></script>
```

In addition to this change, we are going to add id attributes to a few other elements. These will be highlighted in bold below.

One of the elements that will be given an **id** is a **main** element, which will be giving this the id **taskPage**. The reason we have added this is to encapsulate all the task related functionality. This ensures this could co-exist in the same Document Object Model as other functionality, and have the functional areas remain separate.

For instance, we may have a second page for managing a calendar, but it could exist in the same HTML page if required. We would then simply replace the header, footer and main elements with the appropriate elements for the new page.

This approach allows us to change page without a browser refresh, and allows for a single-page web application (SPA). With a single-page application, all content needed by the entire web-application is loaded on the initial request (or with subsequent AJAX calls), and from that point forward content is swapped in and out of the DOM to simulate page changes.

The entire HTML page should now look like this:

```
<!DOCTYPE html>
<html lang="en">
<head>
<meta charset="utf-8">
<title>Task list</title>
<link rel="stylesheet" type="text/css" href="styles/tasks.css"
    media="screen" />
<script src="scripts/jquery-2.0.3.js"></script>
<script src="scripts/jquery-tmpl.js"></script>
<script src="scripts/jquery-serialization.js"></script>
<script src="scripts/tasks-controller.js"></script>
</head>
<body>
    <header>
        <span>Task list</span>
    </header>
    <main  id="taskPage">
    <section id="taskCreation" class="not">
        <form id="taskForm">
            <div>
                <label>Task</label> <input type="text"
required="required"
                name="task" class="large" placeholder="Breakfast at
Tiffanys" />
            </div>
            <div>
                <label>Required by</label> <input type="date"
required="required"
                name="requiredBy" />
            </div>
            <div>
                <label>Category</label> <select name="category">
```

136

```
                    <option value="Personal">Personal</option>
                    <option value="Work">Work</option>
                </select>
            </div>
            <nav>
                <a href="#" id="saveTask">Save task</a>
                <a href="#" id="clearTask">Clear task</a>
            </nav>
        </form>
    </section>
    <section>
        <table id="tblTasks">
            <colgroup>
                <col width="40%">
                <col width="15%">
                <col width="15%">
                <col width="30%">
            </colgroup>
            <thead>
                <tr>
                    <th>Name</th>
                    <th>Due</th>
                    <th>Category</th>
                    <th>Actions</th>
                </tr>
            </thead>
            <tbody>
            </tbody>
        </table>
        <nav>
            <a href="#" id="btnAddTask">Add task</a>
        </nav>
    </section>
</main>
```

```
    <footer>You have 3 tasks</footer>
</body>
<script>
$(document).ready(function() {
    $('[required="required"]').prev('label').
        append( '<span>*</span>').
        children( 'span').addClass('required');
    $('tbody tr:even').addClass('even');

    $('#btnAddTask').click(function(evt) {
        evt.preventDefault();
        $('#taskCreation').removeClass('not');
    });

    $('tbody tr').click(function(evt) {
        $(evt.target).closest('td' ).siblings().
            andSelf().toggleClass('rowHighlight');
    });

    $('#tblTasks tbody').on('click', '.deleteRow', function(evt) {
        evt.preventDefault();
        $(evt.target).parents('tr').remove();
    });

    $('#saveTask').click(function(evt) {
        evt.preventDefault();
        var task = $('form').toObject();
        $('#taskRow').tmpl(task).appendTo($('#tblTasks tbody'));
    });
});
</script>

<script id="taskRow" type="text/x-jQuery-tmpl">
<tr>
```

```
<td>${task}</td>
<td><time datetime="${requiredBy}"> ${requiredBy}</time></td>
<td>${category}</td>
<td>
    <nav>
        <a href="#">Edit</a>
        <a href="#">Complete</a>
        <a href="#" class="deleteRow">Delete</a>
    </nav>
</td>
</tr>
</script>

</html>
```

And the project structure will look as follows:

▼ 🗂 scripts
    📄 jquery-2.0.3.js
    📄 jquery-serialization.js
    📄 jquery-tmpl.js
    📄 tasks-controller.js
▼ 🗂 styles
    📄 tasks.css
📄 tasks.html

We now want to start writing the code for tasks-controller.js. This will utilize the module pattern introduced earlier in the JavaScript chapter. This will ensure the controller can encapsulate data, and expose a public API to the rest of the application.

The controller will be responsible for initializing the form, handling events, and managing any state required by the page. The basic structure of our tasks controller is as follows:

```
tasksController = function() {
  return {
    init : function(page) {


    }
  }
```

```
}();
```

This code is implementing exactly the same pattern as was implemented earlier with the **createIncrementer** function. The only difference here is that we have not named the function that is returning the object: it is an anonymous function that we are executing immediately by adding **()** to the end of the line.

It is important that you understand the impact of the **()** at the end of this code block. It means that the variable represented by **tasksController** is set to the object returned by the anonymous function, not the function itself.

The main advantage of this approach is that no other code can construct another **tasksController**, since there is no function that can be invoked. As a result, the variable **tasksController** is a singleton. A singleton is another design pattern that is used to ensure only a single instance of a type of object (in traditional object orientated languages, only a single instance of a class) will exist in the application.

It is important that our **tasksController** is a singleton, since it is going to manage state. If multiple **tasksController** were created they may have different state, and would therefore interfere with each other when they attempted to update the DOM with this state.

The controller will have a method called **init** that will be responsible for performing any initialization tasks that need to occur when tasks.html loads, but this will be called explicitly within tasks.html rather than implicitly when the script loads. This is because we may have multiple controllers for different functional areas, and we only want to initialize them when the user selects to use them.

When we initialize the controller we are going to pass it the **main** element in tasks.html page as a parameter, This controller is going to be responsible for that specific portion of the DOM, and therefore any jQuery selects it performs should be done within the context of that element.

This is not going to be important in this application, since it will only consist of a single distinct set of functionality, however in a large scale single-page application, with many functional areas, each functional area would be given its own controller, and its own **main** element that it is responsible for.

The following is our controller implementation:

```
tasksController = function() {

  var taskPage;
  var initialised = false;


  return {
    init : function(page) {
      if (!initialised) {
        taskPage = page;
        $(taskPage).find( '[required="required"]' ).
            prev('label').append( '<span>*</span>').
```

```
        children( 'span').addClass('required');
    $(taskPage).find('tbody tr:even').addClass('even');


    $(taskPage).find( '#btnAddTask').click( function(evt) {
        evt.preventDefault();
        $(taskPage ).find('#taskCreation' ).removeClass('not');
    });
    $(taskPage).find('tbody tr' ).click(function(evt) {
    $(evt.target ).closest('td').siblings( ).
        andSelf().toggleClass('rowHighlight');
      });
      $(taskPage ).find('#tblTasks tbody').on('click',
          '.deleteRow', function(evt) {
        evt.preventDefault();
        $(evt.target ).parents('tr').remove();
      });
      $(taskPage).find( '#saveTask' ).click(function(evt) {
        evt.preventDefault();
        var task = $('form').toObject();
        $('#taskRow').tmpl( task).appendTo(
          $(taskPage ).find('#tblTasks tbody'));
        });
      initialised = true;
    }
  }
 }
}();
```

There are a number of features about this controller that should be explained.

Firstly, the controller is storing the page parameter in a local variable called **taskPage**. This variable is hidden from the outside world using the data hiding approach discussed in earlier chapters. This means it is not possible for any other code to change the context that this controller is working within.

Whenever the controller needs to access an HTML element, it does so in the context of this page using the following approach:

```
$(taskPage).find(..)
```

This ensures that even if the HTML page contains other elements with the same properties as the elements on our page, they will not be returned in any jQuery selections.

Secondly, the **taskController** remembers if it has been initialized in a local variable called **initialised**. This ensures that regardless of how many times the **init** method is called, it will only actually initilaize the controller once.

With the controller in place, tasks.html needs to be altered to invoke the **init** method when the page is loaded. The script block in tasks.html should now contain the following:

```
<script>

    $(document).ready(function() {

      tasksController.init($('#taskPage'));

    });

</script>
```

Validation

The next feature that we will add is an essential feature of any form based web application: form validation.

JavaScript has been used to perform field validation since it first appeared in browsers; in fact it was probably the feature JavaScript was used for the most in its early years.

Client side validation remains an important use for JavaScript, but as mentioned earlier in the book, HTML5 now contains a specification for form validation based on form attributes. This validation is intended to remove the need for JavaScript validation.

Although it may not be obvious, this has actually been implemented by default by adding the **required** attribute to our input fields. If you press enter in the "Task" field without entering any input you should see the following:

Task

Breakfast at Tiffanys

⚠ Please fill out this field.

Category

Personal

The message "Please fill out this field" is generated by HTML5 validation.

Despite the presence of HTML5 validation, we will not use it in this web application for two main reasons:

1. All browsers do not support HTML5 validation; therefore it is necessary to rely on a polyfill

for browsers that do not provide support.

2. HTML5 validation does not play as nicely with JavaScript as you would expect. For instance, we can not cause the HTML5 validators to fire by calling submit() in JavaScript, they will only fire if the user clicks a submit button to post data to the server, or on a field by field basis when the user presses enter in the field. Since we will never post data to the server this is not helpful.

For these reasons, we will use the jQuery Validation library in this application. This can be downloaded from here:

http://jqueryvalidation.org/

or is available from the following CDN:

http://ajax.aspnetcdn.com/ajax/jquery.validate/1.11.1/jquery.validate.js

I have downloaded version 1.11.1 and added it to my scripts folder under the name jquery.validate.js. I have also added it to the head section of the web page:

```
<head>
<meta charset="utf-8">
<title>Task list</title>
<link rel="stylesheet" type="text/css" href="styles/tasks.css"
    media="screen" />
<script src="scripts/jquery-2.0.3.js"></script>
<script src="scripts/jquery-tmpl.js"></script>
<script src="scripts/jquery.validate.js"></script>
<script src="scripts/jquery-serialization.js"></script>
<script src="scripts/tasks-controller.js"></script>
</head>
```

Fortunately, jQuery validation relies on the same attributes as HTML5 where possible, so the **required** attributes are valid for both HTML5 and jQuery validation.

jQuery validation contains a large number of built in validators, these allow you to express rules for:

- Validating a required field has a value.

- Validating a field contains a number.

- Validating the length of input data.

- Validating a number is in a range.

- Validating a field contains an email address.

- Validating a field contains a possibly valid credit card number.

In addition to these default validators; you can add your own validators.

In order to implement jQuery validation, we are first going to change the input field with the name "task" to include a maximum length:

```
<input type="text" required="required" maxlength="200" name="task"
class="large" placeholder="Breakfast at Tiffanys"/>
```

Next we are going to change the event listener that is invoked when "Save Task" is invoked. This will check whether the form is valid by calling the **valid** function on it. As you have probably guessed, this is a function that has been added to jQuery by the jQuery Validation plugin. The actual saving of the task will only occur if the form is valid:

```
$(taskPage).find('#saveTask').click(function(evt) {

  evt.preventDefault();

  if ($(taskPage).find('form').valid()) {

    var task = $('form').toObject();

    $('#taskRow').tmpl(task ).appendTo($(taskPage ).find('#tblTasks
tbody'));

  }

});
```

If you now attempt to save a task without including mandatory fields, error messages will be generated:

```
Task*

Breakfast at Tiffanys

This field is required.

Required by*

dd/mm/yyyy          ▼

This field is required.
```

In order to see the elements that jQuery Validation has added, highlight the text that says "This field is required", right click on the text, and choose "Inspect element": you should see the following:

```
<form id="taskform" novalidate="novalidate">
▼<div>
    <label for="task">Task</label>
    <input type="text" required="required" maxlength="200" name="task" class="lar
    <label for="task" class="error" style>This field is required.</label>
  </div>
▶<div>...</div>
▶<div>...</div>
```

jQuery Validation has added a label with the class of error. This has then been rendered in bold, red text by the following class in tasks.css:

```
label.error {
```

```
  color: red;
   font-weight:bold;
}
```

Conclusion

The web application is still far from complete at this stage, but the basic project structure is now in place. Before adding additional functionality we are going to pause and begin implementing the functionality to store the application's data and resources inside the browser.

10 MANAGING CLIENT-SIDE DATA

Although we have aspects of a working web application, clearly there is a major flaw in the current implementation: every time the user refreshes the tasks.html page all the tasks are lost.

In this section we are going to examine ways in which we can maintain the state of the application (the tasks) between page refreshes without utilizing server side storage.

Traditionally the only mechanism for storing data on the client in a way that survives page refreshes was cookies. A cookie is a simple text based name/value pair that is stored on the client. The server can set a cookie on the client by including it in an HTTP response.

Every-time the browser sends an HTTP request to the domain from this point forward, the cookie (both its name and value) will be included in the request.

Cookies can also be created and interacted with (with some restrictions) using JavaScript.

Cookies are great for managing some data. For instance, it is common for web sites to store a session ID in a cookie to represent each user's individual session. This allows the server to differentiate each unique session, and keep them separate. This is essential, since HTTP is a stateless protocol, and there is no other inherent way to know that two HTTP requests are actually from the same browser session.

While cookies are great for storing simple data on the client, they are not great for storing large amounts of data such as our task list. Cookies have significant limitations that make them inappropriate for storing large amounts of data:

1. They are included on each request to the server, so unless you want the entire task list to be included on each request, cookies are not a good solution.

2. The maximum size of each cookie is approximately 5 kilobytes.

3. The maximum number of cookies that a single domain can store is 20 (this can be browser dependent). This means that the total amount of cookie storage available to a domain is less than 100 kilobytes.

It has therefore been evident for some time that HTML needs some form of offline data storage if it is to allow for rich and dynamic web applications that can exist independent of a web server. Even applications that are continually connected to a web server can significantly improve user experiences if they could cache larger quantities of data in the browser.

There are now three distinct APIs for storing data on the client, all of which fall within the umbrella of HTML5.

• Web storage: this is the simplest form of offline storage and supports name/value pairs where the name and value must both be strings. Although this is a relatively simple storage mechanism, and does come with a number of limitations, all major web browsers support it.

• Web SQL Database API: this API supports a relational database within the browser (similar to MySQL). Although this has many advantages, particularly for developers already familiar with relational databases and SQL, Chrome and IE have announced that they will never support this API, therefore it is effectively dead.

• IndexedDB: (formerly WebSimpleDB) this API exposes an object store. Objects (or simple data types) can be stored against a key, and retrieved either through this key, or other indexes added to the record. IndexedDB supports a transactional model familiar to database developers, but does not include a generic query language such as SQL. This is a promising API, but is not yet supported by all browsers. In particular, Safari, and some mobile browsers do not support this API.

In this chapter we will create a storage API that allows us to abstract the underlying storage API from the web application. This means that the web application will not be aware which underlying API it is using, which then allows the most appropriate API to be used (depending on browser support).

This approach is another example of a design pattern called the bridge pattern.

This chapter will provide implementations for both Web storage and IndexedDB. We will refer to the persistence layer API as a "storage engine".

Storage Engine API

Our storage engine API will be capable of performing all the basic CRUD operations:

• Create

• Read

• Update

• Delete

The API will operate on JavaScript objects. The only constraint that will be placed on an object to be storable is that it must have a property called **id**, which will be unique within the specific type of object (e.g. tasks).

All objects will be stored according to their defined type; for instance, tasks will be stored under the type of "task". If the data store did not have a concept of object-type it would not be able to differentiate related and unrelated objects, and all objects would need to be stored together. For instance, if the web application supported calendar events and tasks, we would want a way of retrieving all the calendar events without retrieving the tasks. It therefore makes sense to store them separate from one another.

Finally, the API will work with callback functions rather than direct return values. When calling an API method, the invoker will pass a success callback function and an error callback function. When the processing completes, one of these callback functions will be invoked, and passed the result of the processing.

The use of callbacks will allow us to support both synchronous and asynchronous storage mechanisms. A synchronous storage mechanism is one that performs storage operations on the main browser thread, and blocks until it is complete. An asynchronous storage mechanism on the other hand may utilize background threads using the Web Worker API that will be introduced in later chapters, or via an AJAX call to the server.

If you are not familiar with callbacks, the examples below will provide a simple introduction. Callbacks will also be used in several other APIs in the chapters that follow.

The section below provides documentation on the API that will be implemented. Up until this point we have largely ignored the importance of well-documented code. The section below therefore also serves as an example of the way an API can be documented to make it usable to an audience beyond its creator:

```
/**

* The client must call this to initialize the storage engine before
using it.

* If the storage engine initializes successfully the successCallback
will be invoked with a null object.

* If the errorCallback is invoked then the storage engine cannot be
used.

* It should be possible to call this method multiple times, and the
same result will be returned each time.

*

* @param {Function} successCallback The callback that will be invoked
if the storage engine initializes.

* @param {Function} errorCallback The callback that will be invoked in
error scenarios.

*/

function init(successCallback, errorCallback)



/**

* The client must call this to initialize a specific object type in the
storage engine.

* If the storage engine supports the object type the successCallback
will be invoked with a null value.

* It should be possible to call this method multiple times, and the
same result will be returned each time.

* If the errorCallback is invoked then the object type cannot be
stored.

*

* @param {String} type The type of object that will be stored.
```

```
* @param {Function} successCallback The callback that will be invoked
if the storage engine initializes.
```

```
* @param {Function} errorCallback The callback that will be invoked on
error scenarios.
```

```
*/
```

```
function initObjectStore(type, successCallback, errorCallback)
```

```
/**
```

```
* This can be used to find all the objects for a specific type.
* If there are no objects found for that type this will return an empty
array.
```

```
*
```

```
* @param {String} type The type of object that should be searched for.
```

```
* @param {Function} successCallback The callback that will be invoked
after the query completes. This will be passed an array of objects
conforming to the requested type.
```

```
* @param {Function} errorCallback The callback that will be invoked on
error scenarios.
```

```
*/
```

```
function findAll(type, successCallback, errorCallback)
```

```
/**
```

```
* This will return an object with a specific id for a specific type.
* If no object is found this will return null
```

```
*
```

```
* @param {String} type The type of object that should be searched for.
```

```
* @param {String|number} id The unique ID of the object
```

```
* @param {Function} successCallback The callback that will be invoked
after the query completes. This will be passed an object conforming to
the requested type or null.
```

```
* @param {Function} errorCallback The callback that will be invoked on
error scenarios.
```

```
*/
```

```
function findById(type, id, successCallback, errorCallback)
```

```
/**

* This will handle adding and editing objects of a specific type.

* If the id property of the object passed in is null or undefined, an
id will be assigned for the object, and it will be saved.
* If the id property is non-null then the object will be updated.
* If the id cannot be found the error callback will be invoked.
* On success, the newly saved object will be returned to the success
callback.

*

* @param {String} type The type of object that will be stored.

* @param {Object} obj The object that will be stored.

* @param {Function} successCallback The callback that will be invoked
after the object has been committed to the storage engine. This will be
the stored object, including the id property.

* @param {Function} errorCallback The callback that will be invoked on
error scenarios.

*/

function save(type, obj, successCallback, errorCallback)


/*
* This will delete an object with a specific id for a specific type.
* If no object exists with that id, the error callback will be invoked.
* If an object is deleted this function will return the id of the
deleted object to the successCallback

*

* @param {String} type The type of object that will be deleted.

* @param {String|number} id The unique id of the object.

* @param {Function} successCallback The callback that will be invoked
after the object has been deleted from the storage engine. This will be
passed the unique id of the deleted object.

* @param {Function} errorCallback The callback that will be invoked on
error scenarios.


*/

function delete(type, id, successCallback, errorCallback)


/**

* This can be used for querying objects based on a property value.
```

```
* A single property name can be passed in, along with the value that
matches. Any objects with that value for the property specified will be
returned.

*

* @param {String} type The type of object that will be searched for.

* @param {String} propertyName The property name to be matched.

* @param {String|number} propertyValue The value that property should
have.

* @param {Function} successCallback The callback that will be invoked
after the query completes. This will be an array of 0 or more objects
of the specified type.

* @param {Function} errorCallback The callback that will be invoked on
error scenarios.

*/
```

function findByProperty(type, propertyName, propertyValue, successCallback, errorCallback)

Finally, we need to define the API for the success and error callbacks. These should be functions, and conform to the following signature:

```
/*

* This will be called in all success scenarios.

* @param {any} result The success result, as documented on individual
method calls.

*/
```

function succcssCallback(result)

```
/*

* This will be called in all failure scenarios.

* @param {String} errorCode The type of exception

* @param {String} errorMessage A human readable version of the error
message.

*/
```

function errorCallback(errorCode, errorMessage)

This simple API is sufficient to perform all our data storage needs.

Web Storage Implementation

In order to see how simple the Web storage API is, open the Chrome console (on any web page) and type the following:

```
> localStorage.setItem('item1', 'This is item 1')
```

This line of code saved the value 'This is item 1' under the key 'item1'. This will now be persisted indefinitely, and available to all pages from the same origin as this page.

In order to prove that this has been persisted, open the "Resources" tab of the Chrome developer tools, and locate "Local Storage" on the left hand side. You should see the following:

| Elements | Resources | Network | Sources | Timeline | Profiles | Audits | Console |

	Key	Value
▼ Frames	item1	This is item 1
▶ (tasks.html)		
▶ Web SQL		
▶ IndexedDB		
▼ Local Storage		
file://		
▶ Session Storage		
▼ Cookies		
Local Files		

If you wish to retrieve this value you can do so with the following call:

```
> localStorage.getItem('item1')
```

And if you want to remove the value you can do so with the following call:

```
> localStorage.removeItem('item1')
```

Or you can completely clear all data stored by this origin with:

```
> localStorage.clear()
```

In addition to the **localStorage** object, the exact same API exists on an object called **sessionStorage**. This performs the same role as **localStorage**, but the data is automatically cleared when the browser is closed. Data in **localStorage** on the other hand is persisted indefinitely, although the user is free to clear it at any time.

Web storage is a simple API, but is limited. For instance, if you try to insert an object into **localStorage** it will appear to succeed:

```
> localStorage.setItem('item1', {})
```

If you retrieve the value back however, you will see that the persisted value is a string: the result of calling **toString** on the object:

```
> localStorage.getItem('item1')
```

```
"[object Object]"
```

Web storage can only be used to store strings. This turns out not to be a huge issue due to the fact we can serialize objects to strings easily with the JSON.stringify() function, and de-serialize them with JSON.parse();

Another limitation of the Web storage API is that storage is limited to 5MB in most browsers. If this limit was not small enough, JavaScript uses UTF-16 as the character encoding for all strings. UTF-16 represents all characters as at least 2 byte (16 bit) sequences. This is a limitation for most Western languages, since other UTF encodings (most notably UTF-8) represent the characters in the Latin alphabet with a single byte.

 The JavaScript specification permits the use of either UTF-16 or UCS-2. UCS-2 was the precursor to UTF-16, and is a fixed length 2-byte encoding. This was superseded as the number of code-points in the Unicode code space grew.

Due to the fact JavaScript uses UTF-16, the amount of character data it can store in 5MB is approximately half the amount as could have been stored with UTF-8 (assuming we are using mainly characters from the Latin alphabet). Effectively this reduces the size of Web storage to 2.5MB: this is still far better than cookies, but is a limitation we need to bear in mind when developing web applications.

I successfully managed to bypass this limit on one project by compressing all data with the LZW compression algorithm. This effectively increased the amount of data that could be stored to 50MB in this particular case (results will vary depending on how repetitive data is).

This page provides implementations of the LZW algorithm in a variety of languages including JavaScript:

http://rosettacode.org/wiki/LZW_compression

The implementation of our storage engine with Web storage will store each type of object in an object of its own called an "object store" (if you are familiar with relational databases, you can think of this object as a table). The properties of the object store will be the **id** property of each object held for that type (the rows in the table), and the value will be the object persisted. This approach relies on the fact that the **id** property of each object must be unique within its type.

The storage engine needs to generate unique IDs for objects. The approach we will use with the Web storage API is to use the current time in milliseconds. This is not a great choice for an **id**, since if two objects could be created in quick enough succession they will get the same **id**. A better approach is to use UUIDs (Universally Unique Identifiers), but we will avoid that complexity for now.

 The most commonly used JavaScript implementation of UUIDs can be found here:

http://www.broofa.com/2008/09/javascript-uuid-function

In order to obtain the current time in milliseconds we can use the jQuery helper:

```
> $.now()
```

The storage engine will be represented by a module. This will not have any dependencies to other code developed for the tasks screen, therefore it is completely reusable by other functionality if required. The module will be stored in a variable called storageEngine.

The storageEngine will be initialized when the tasks.html page loads, and will be available for use by the **tasksController**, or any other JavaScript code, since the storageEngine variable is bound to the global **window** object.

Begin by creating a JavaScript file called tasks-webstorage.js in the scripts folder. Next, import this into tasks.html:

```
<script src="scripts/tasks-webstorage.js"></script>
```

The code below is the initial version of the storageEngine module. This provides the basic structure for the module, along with implementations of **init** and **initObjectStore**:

```
storageEngine = function() {
  var initialized = false;
  var initializedObjectStores = {};
  return {
    init : function(successCallback, errorCallback) {
      if (window.localStorage) {
        initialized = true;
        successCallback(null);
      } else {
        errorCallback('storage_api_not_supported',
            'The web storage api is not supported');
      }
    },
    initObjectStore : function(type, successCallback, errorCallback) {
      if (!initialized) {
        errorCallback('storage_api_not_initialized',
            'The storage engine has not been initialized');
      } else if (!localStorage.getItem(type)) {
        localStorage.setItem(type, JSON.stringify({}));
      }
      initializedObjectStores[type] = true;
      successCallback(null);
    },
```

```
    save : function(type, obj, successCallback, errorCallback) {

    },

    findAll : function(type, successCallback, errorCallback) {

    },

    delete : function(type, id, successCallback, errorCallback) {

    },

    findByProperty : function(type, propertyName, propertyValue,
            successCallback, errorCallback) {

    },

    findById : function (type, id, successCallback, errorCallback){

    }

  }

}();
```

Like the **tasksController**, this controller implicitly creates a new object. The object in this case will be stored in a global variable called **storageEngine**.

The initial implementation above contains implementations of the **init** and **initObjectStore** methods. Technically the Web storage implementation does not need the **init** method, since there is nothing that specifically needs initializing in order to use the **localStorage** object. This method has been added to the API however, since it is common for other storage APIs to require initialization before use.

The **init** method simply checks that the **localStorage** object is available in the browser. If it is available, it sets a variable in the storage engine called **initialised** to **true**. Due to the specification of the API, the other methods of the Web storage implementation will not be able to be invoked unless this method has been called.

The **initObjectStore** method checks to see whether the **localStorage** object currently contains an item for the **type** passed in (e.g. "tasks"). If not, it creates an empty object in **localStorage** using the **type** as the key for the item. It will also keep track of the fact that we have initialized this object store.

If you reload tasks.html, the following can be executed from the command line to initialize the storage engine:

```
> storageEngine.init(function(){
    console.log('Storage is initialised');
  },
  function(errorCode, errorMessage) {
    console.log(errorCode+':'+errorMessage);
  }
);
```

The **init** method is passed two functions for the success and error callbacks respectively. When invoked, these functions simply log the fact that they have been called. This call should result in the following being printed to the console:

```
"Storage is initialized"
```

Likewise, the **iniObjectStore** method can be invoked as follows:

```
> storageEngine.iniObjectStore('testing',
    function(){
      console.log('New type added');
    },
    function(errorCode, errorMessage) {
      console.log(errorCode+':'+errorMessage);
    }
);
```

```
New type added
```

This call will create a new object store called **testing**, and then invoke the success callback which will log success to the console. After invoking this, the **testing** item will be available in localStorage. This can be verified using the shortcut:

```
> localStorage.testing
```

```
"{}"
```

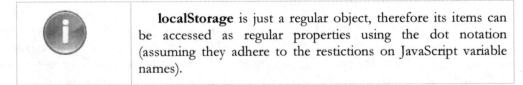

localStorage is just a regular object, therefore its items can be accessed as regular properties using the dot notation (assuming they adhere to the restictions on JavaScript variable names).

An important feature of both the **init** and **initObjectStore** methods is that they can be invoked multiple times and will always return the same output for the same inputs. This is an important feature, since a client may not know if these have been called by other code. Rather than requiring the client to find out whether the initialization has occurred, and call **init** if it hasn't, the client can simply call **init** and have it take care of the logic of working out what needs to be done.

The **tasksController** will be responsible for calling **init** and **initObjectStore**. Before providing the implementation to call the initialization methods, it is worth thinking about the error callback. Every time a storage engine method is invoked, an error callback must be provided.

We will therefore create a generic function that can be used for the **errorCallback**, and store this as a private variable in **tasksController**. All this will do is log the fact that an error has occurred, but if we want to change the behavior, we would be able to do so in a single place, rather than changing all the error callbacks.

The function can be added as a private function within **tasksController**:

```
tasksController = function() {
  function errorLogger(errorCode, errorMessage) {
    console.log(errorCode +':'+ errorMessage);
  }
```

Next, at the start of the **init** method in **tasksController**, add the following code:

```
storageEngine.init(function() {
  storageEngine.initObjectStore('task', function() {


  }, errorLogger)
}, errorLogger);
```

This code calls the **init** method on the storage engine, and when that succeeds, the success callback is invoked, which in turn calls the **initObjectStore** method. This fulfills an important need: since the **init** success callback may not be called immediately in other implementations of this API (i.e. those that perform their processing asynchronously), it is necessary to ensure that **init** succeeds before calling the **initObjectStore** method. If we did not do this, we may call **initObjectStore** while **init** was still processing.

This highlights the challenge of working with interfaces that can perform asynchronous processing. It is often necessary to chain together a whole set of function calls, each inside the callback of its predecessor. This makes code less elegant than the "chaining" approach we saw with jQuery.

We will next implement the first interesting method of the storage engine: the **save** method. Add the following as a new public method to the **storageEngine** module:

```
save: function(type, obj, successCallback, errorCallback) {
  if (!initialized) {
    errorCallback('storage_api_not_initialized',
        'The storage engine has not been initialized');
  } else if (!initializedObjectStores[type]) {
    errorCallback('store_not_initialized',
        'The object store '+type+' has not been initialized');
  }
  if (!obj.id) {
    obj.id = $.now();
  }
  var savedTypeString = localStorage.getItem(type);
```

```
var storageItem = JSON.parse(savedTypeString);
storageItem[obj.id] = obj;
localStorage.setItem(type, JSON.stringify(storageItem));
successCallback(obj);
}
```

As discussed above, this function accepts four parameters. When we invoke this from our task application, the first parameter will always be "task", while the second parameter will be an object representing a task. The third and forth parameters are the success and error callbacks respectively.

Let's step through this implementation line by line.

The first block of code simply checks that **init** and **initObjectStore** have been invoked. If these have not been invoked, the error callback is invoked:

```
if (!initialized) {
  errorCallback('storage_api_not_initialized',
     'The storage engine has not been initialized');
} else if (!initializedObjectStores[type]) {
  errorCallback('store_not_initialized',
    'The object store '+type+' has not been initialized');
}
```

The next section of the method checks if the object to be saved has an **id** or not: if it does not have an **id**, a unique **id** is assigned.

```
if (!obj.id) {
  obj.id = $.now();
}
```

We next query **localStorage** for the relevant object store (e.g. "task"). Since **initObjectStore** has been invoked we can guarantee that there will be an object for the specified **type**:

```
var savedTypeString = localStorage.getItem(type);
```

Next, we de-serialize the "stringified" version of the object store back into an object:

```
var storageItem = JSON.parse(savedTypeString);
```

We then add the object to be saved to the object store, using the **id** property of the object as the property name. This will overwrite a value if it is already there, which means the same code handles creates and updates:

```
storageItem[obj.id] = obj;
```

Also notice that we are not using the dot notation. Since the id starts with a number, it is not a valid JavaScript variable name, and therefore the dot notation would not work.

We then serialize **storedItem** back into a string and add it back into **localStorage**:

```
localStorage.setItem(type, JSON.stringify(storageItem));
```

This will automatically update the item stored against this key.

Finally, the success callback is invoked with the newly saved object:

```
successCallback(obj);
```

With the save method implemented, we can alter the save task event listener in tasks-controller.js to utilize the method:

```
$(taskPage).find('#saveTask').click(function(evt) {
    evt.preventDefault();
    if ($(taskPage).find('form').valid()) {
        var task = $('form').toObject();
        storageEngine.save('task', task,
            function(savedTask) {
                $('#taskRow').tmpl( savedTask).appendTo(
                    $(taskPage).find( '#tblTasks tbody'));
            }, errorLogger);
    }
});
```

Notice that we only update the table in the **successCallback**. This ensures that we do not update the screen unless the actual save is successful.

If you now create a task, you should see the following in the Chrome resources tab:

The next method we will implement is **findAll**. Before adding this, we will provide a helper for obtaining the de-serialized object for a specified type. This will preform the de-serialization logic for us. This can be added as a private function at the top of **storageEngine**.

```
storageEngine = function() {
    var initialized = false;
    var initializedObjectStores = {};
    function getStorageObject(type) {
        var item = localStorage.getItem(type);
        var parsedItem = JSON.parse(item);
        return parsedItem;
```

```
}
```

The following lines in the save method:

```
var savedTypeString = localStorage.getItem(type);
var storageItem = JSON.parse(savedTypeString);
storageItem[obj.id] = obj;
localStorage.setItem(type, JSON.stringify(storageItem));
successCallback(obj);
```

can now be changed to:

```
var storageItem = getStorageObject(type);
storageItem[obj.id] = obj;
localStorage.setItem(type, JSON.stringify(storageItem));
successCallback(obj);
```

The **findAll** method will allow us to repopulate the saved tasks from **localStorage** back into the **table** when the page is refreshed. The following is the implementation of **findAll**:

```
findAll : function(type, successCallback, errorCallback) {
  if (!initialized) {
    errorCallback('storage_api_not_initialized',
        'The storage engine has not been initialized');
  } else if (!initializedObjectStores[type]) {
    errorCallback(store_not_initialized',
        'The object store '+type+' has not been initialized');
  }
  var result = [];
  var storageItem = getStorageObject(type);
  $.each(storageItem, function(i, v) {
    result.push(v);
  });
  successCallback(result);
}
```

Again, we will step through the implementation line by line.

The first section of the method performs the same checks as the **save** method in order to check **init** and **initObjectStore** have both been invoked.

Next, we initialize an array to return the objects available for the specified type. This ensures even if there are no saved objects an empty array will be returned:

```
var result = [];
```

We then use the helper function to return the object store for the specified type:

```
var storageItem = getStorageObject(type);
```

The object store will contain a set of properties representing all the saved objects for this type, therefore we iterate through them and add each value to the results array using the **push** method:

```
$.each(storageItem, function(i, v) {
  result.push(v);
});
```

The result is then returned to the success callback:

```
successCallback(result);
```

The **findAll** method can now be invoked from the tasks-controller.js file. The functionality to call **findAll** and add all the results to the table will be included in a new public method after the **init** method called **loadTasks**:

```
loadTasks : function() {
  storageEngine.findAll('task', function(tasks) {
    $.each(tasks, function(index, task) {
      $('#taskRow').tmpl(task ).appendTo($(taskPage).find( '#tblTasks
tbody'));
    });
  }, errorLogger);
}
```

This performs the call to **findAll**, and then, in the success callback, iterates through the results one by one and adds them to the table using the template.

Now, inside the tasks.html page, add a call to this method after the call to **init**:

```
$(document).ready(function() {
  tasksController.init($('#taskPage'));
  tasksController.loadTasks();
})
```

If you reload tasks.html, any saved tasks should load into the table.

We can now add the **delete** method to the storage engine.

```
delete : function(type, id, successCallback, errorCallback) {
  if (!initialized) {
    errorCallback('storage_api_not_initialized',
      'The storage engine has not been initialized');
  } else if (!initializeObjectStores[type]) {
```

```
    errorCallback('store_not_initialized',
        'The object store '+type+' has not been initialized');
  }
  var storageItem = getStorageObject(type);
  if (storageItem[id]) {
    delete storageItem[id];
    localStorage.setItem(type, JSON.stringify(storageItem));
     successCallback(id);
  }
  errorCallback("object_not_found",
        "The object requested could not be found");
}
```

The delete implementation is straightforward; the one aspect that may be new is the line:

```
delete storageItem[id];
```

It is possible to delete a property (and therefore its value) from an object by using the delete keyword. Since we are storing each item as a property of an object, we can delete the individual items with this technique. After invoking this, the property specified is **undefined**.

When the delete button is clicked we need to know which task needs to be deleted. We therefore need to update the delete button on screen so that it knows which task it relates to, therefore change the following line in the template:

```
<a href="#" class="deleteRow">Delete</a>
```

to

```
<a href="#" class="deleteRow" data-task-id="${id}">Delete</a>
```

This uses a custom data attribute to keep track of which task each delete button is responsible for.

Now change the delete implementation in tasks-controller.js from this:

```
$(taskPage).find('#tblTasks tbody').on('click', '.deleteRow',
    function(evt) {
        $(evt.target).parents('tr').remove();
});
```

to this:

```
$(taskPage).find('#tblTasks tbody').on('click', '.deleteRow',
  function(evt) {
    storageEngine.delete('task',  $(evt.target).data().taskId,
        function() {
```

```
        $(evt.target).parents('tr').remove();
    }, errorLogger);

}
);
```

When any delete button is clicked, the element that was clicked is available in $(evt.target). We then use the HTML5 data() function to obtain all the data attributes associated with the element. This extracts all the attributes that begin with "data-" and makes them available in an object, where each property in the object represents one of the data attributes.

You may have noticed that the attribute "data-task-id" is available as data().taskId. Since attribute names are converted to lower case inside the DOM, hyphens are typically used to separate words in attribute names. In JavaScript, the common convention is to separate words through the use of capitalization. The data() object therefore converts attribute names into forms more conventional for use in JavaScript.

The data attribute could have also been retrieved with the following call:

```
$(evt.target).attr('data-task-id');
```

Also note that we only update the table once we know that the storage engine has successfully deleted the row. This ensures that if there is an error during the processing, the screen does not get out of sync with the storage engine.

If you now delete a row, and refresh the page, you will see the task has been permanently deleted.

Finally, we will add the two remaining functions to the **storageEngine**:

```
findByProperty : function(type, propertyName, propertyValue,
successCallback, errorCallback) {
    if (!initialized) {
        errorCallback('storage_api_not_initialized',
            'The storage engine has not been initialized');
    } else if (!initializedObjectStores[type]) {
        errorCallback('store_not_initialized',
            'The object store '+type+' has not been initialized');
    }
    var result = [];
    var storageItem = getStorageObject(type);
    $.each(storageItem, function(i, v) {
        if (v[propertyName] === propertyValue) {
            result.push(v);
        }
    });
```

```
    successCallback(result);
},
findById : function (type, id, successCallback, errorCallback)     {
  if (!initialized) {
    errorCallback('storage_api_not_initialized',
        'The storage engine has not been initialized');
  } else if (!initializedObjectStores[type]) {
    errorCallback('store_not_initialized',
          'The object store '+type+' has not been initialized');
  }
  var storageItem = getStorageObject(type);
  var result = storageItem[id];
  successCallback(result);
}
```

The implementations of these methods should now look fairly straightforward. They are continuing the same pattern of obtaining the object store, and accessing the relevant items from this to return to the client.

With all the pieces of the storage engine in place, we can add "edit" functionality to the application. This will allow tasks to be updated after they have been created. This will utilize the same form as the one used to add tasks, therefore the form needs to contain a hidden field to capture the existing id of an object if there is one:

```
<form id="taskForm">
    <input type="hidden" name="id"/>
```

This will allow us to serialize and de-serialize all properties of the task, not just the visible properties.

Next, change the edit button in the template from this:

```
<a href="#">Edit</a>
```

to this:

```
<a href="#" class="editRow" data-task-id="${id}">Edit</a>
```

This is following the same pattern that was established with the delete button.

With this in place, we can add an event listener in the **init** method of tasks-controller.js. When the user clicks to edit a task in the table, the task will be retrieved from the storage engine using the **findById** method. It will then be loaded into the form using the serialization plugin we wrote earlier in the book:

```
$(taskPage).find('#tblTasks tbody').on('click', '.editRow',
  function(evt) {
```

```
$(taskPage).find('#taskCreation').removeClass('not');
storageEngine.findById('task', $(evt.target).data().taskId,
    function(task) {
        $(taskPage).find('form').fromObject(task);
    }, errorLogger);
  }
);
```

With this in place, the existing **save** method can remain unchanged, since it was already designed to handle updates. The task that is passed to the save method on an edit will contain an **id** property, and therefore an update will be performed.

We do not have code in place however to update the table after the edit has occurred – the current functionality will simply add a new row after the edit. We will therefore change it to this:

```
$(taskPage).find('#saveTask').click(function(evt) {
  evt.preventDefault();
  if ($(taskPage).find('form').valid()) {
    var task = $(taskPage).find('form').toObject();
    storageEngine.save('task', task, function() {
      $(taskPage).find('#tblTasks tbody').empty();
      tasksController.loadTasks();
      $(':input').val('');
      $(taskPage).find('#taskCreation' ).addClass('not');
    }, errorLogger);
  }
});
```

This will now empty and recreate the tasks table when a task is saved. If there was going to be a large number of tasks we would probably look at producing a more optimized implementation that simply updated the correct row, but it is best to start simple, and optimize if required.

There is a famous quote by Donald Knuth:

"We should forget about small efficiencies, say about 97% of the time: premature optimization is the root of all evil".

This functionality will also clear the input fields and hide the edit portion of the screen. This ensures that if a user clicks the "Add task" button, the fields will not be prepopulated with data from the previous edit.

The final version of the Web storage based storage engine should be as follows:

```
storageEngine = function() {
```

```
var initialized = false;
var initializedObjectStores = {};
function getStorageObject(type) {
  var item = localStorage.getItem(type);
  var parsedItem = JSON.parse(item);
  return parsedItem;
}
return {
init : function(successCallback, errorCallback) {
  if (window.localStorage) {
  initialized = true;
  successCallback(null);
    } else {
      errorCallback('storage_api_not_supported',
        'The web storage api is not supported');
    }
  },
  initObjectStore : function(type, successCallback, errorCallback) {
    if (!initialized) {
      errorCallback('storage_api_not_initialized',
        'The storage engine has not been initialized');
    } else if (!localStorage.getItem(type)) {
      localStorage.setItem(type, JSON.stringify({}));
    }
    initializedObjectStores[type] = true;
    successCallback(null);
  },
  save: function(type, obj, successCallback, errorCallback) {
    if (!initialized) {
        errorCallback('storage_api_not_initialized',
          'The storage engine has not been initialized');
    } else if (!initializedObjectStores[type]) {
      errorCallback('store_not_initialized',
          'The object store '+type+' has not been initialized');
```

```
      }
      if (!obj.id) {
        obj.id = $.now();
      }
      var storageItem = getStorageObject(type);
      storageItem[obj.id] = obj;
      localStorage.setItem(type, JSON.stringify(storageItem));
      successCallback(obj);
    },
    findAll : function(type, successCallback, errorCallback) {
      if (!initialized) {
        errorCallback('storage_api_not_initialized',
          'The storage engine has not been initialized');
      } else if (!initializedObjectStores[type]) {
        errorCallback('store_not_initialized',
          'The object store '+type+' has not been initialized');
      }
      var result = [];
      var storageItem = getStorageObject(type);
      $.each(storageItem, function(i, v) {
        result.push(v);
      });
      successCallback(result);
    },
    delete : function(type, id, successCallback, errorCallback) {
      if (!initialized) {
        errorCallback('storage_api_not_initialized',
          'The storage engine has not been initialized');
      } else if (!initializedObjectStores[type]) {
        errorCallback('store_not_initialized',
          'The object store '+type+' has not been initialized');
      }
      var storageItem = getStorageObject(type);
      if (storageItem[id]) {
```

```
        delete storageItem[id];
        localStorage.setItem(type, JSON.stringify(storageItem));
        successCallback(id);
    } else {
    errorCallback("object_not_found",
        "The object requested could not be found");
    }
},
    findByProperty : function(type, propertyName, propertyValue,
successCallback, errorCallback) {
    if (!initialized) {
        errorCallback('storage_api_not_initialized',
        'The storage engine has not been initialized');
    } else if (!initializedObjectStores[type]) {
        errorCallback('store_not_initialized',
            'The object store '+type+' has not been initialized');
    }
    var result = [];
    var storageItem = getStorageObject(type);
    $.each(storageItem, function(i, v) {
        if (v[propertyName] === propertyValue) {
            result.push(v);
        }
    });
    successCallback(result);
},
    findById : function (type, id, successCallback, errorCallback)  {
    if (!initialized) {
        errorCallback('storage_api_not_initialized',
            'The storage engine has not been initialized');
    } else if (!initializedObjectStores[type]) {
        errorCallback('store_not_initialized',
            'The object store '+type+' has not been initialized');
    }
```

```
        var storageItem = getStorageObject(type);

        var result = storageItem[id];

        successCallback(result);

    }


    }

}();
```

There are definite pros and cons to using the Web storage API. The main advantage is that it is supported in all major browsers, and is extremely simple to use.

The main disadvantages with the Web storage API would only become apparent if we needed to support a large amount of data. Not only does Web Storage only support a maximum of 5MB data in some browsers, even where it does support larger limits, accessing a minimal data set from a large data set may be time consuming, since there is no query API for accessing data. Data access is fast when it is based on the item's key, but slow in any other scenario.

There are two other disadvantages with the Web storage API.

Firstly, it does not support transactions. In our simple cases this has not been an issue, but if we wanted to be able to save multiple tasks, and have them all either succeed (commit), or all fail (rollback), we would need to write our own custom code to handle this. This would need to use "compensating transactions": if a change failed after other changes had succeeded, we would need to write custom code to undo the earlier changes.

Secondly, the Web storage API is a synchronous API and operates on the main browser thread. Again, this is not an issue for small data sets, but could become an issue with large data sets.

The API we will look at in the next section resolves these issues, but does so at the cost of additional complexity.

IndexedDB Implementation

We will now implement the storage engine using the IndexedDB API. Due to the fact we are using the same API we will not need to change anything else in our application. The tasks-controller.js does not care how the storage engine is implemented, only that the API behaves as advertised.

IndexedDB is a more sophisticated API than Web storage. Although it is an object database rather than a classic relational database, it incorporates concepts that are familiar to those who have worked with relational databases, such as transactions and indexes.

IndexedDB always operates with asynchronous callbacks, but by default it does still use the main browser thread. It is also possible for browser vendors to implement the IndexedDB API with Web Workers (a subject that will be introduced in later chapters), which allows processing to occur on a separate thread.

Not all major browsers currently support IndexedDB. In addition, some browsers do not support it through the "indexedDB" object, only through a vendor named object (e.g. mozIndexedDB in Firefox, msIndexedDB in IE). This is used to indicate that the browser does not provide full compliance with the specification. The implementation below will ignore these alternatively named implementations.

To begin implementing the API, create a new file in the scripts folder called tasks-indexeddb.js. Inside this add the skeleton of our API:

```
storageEngine = function() {

return {

    init : function(successCallback, errorCallback) {

    },

     initObjectStore : function(type, successCallback, errorCallback) {

     },

    save : function(type, obj, successCallback, errorCallback) {

    },

    findAll : function(type, successCallback, errorCallback) {

    },

    delete : function(type, id, successCallback, errorCallback) {

    },

    findByProperty : function(type, propertyName, propertyValue,
successCallback, errorCallback) {

    },

    findById : function (type, id, successCallback, errorCallback)  {

    }

  }

}();
```

In addition, comment out the tasks-webstorage.js from the tasks.html page and add in tasks-indexeddb.js in its place. We will eventually move to a model where the browser will choose the best implementation, but for now we will concentrate on getting the **IndexedDB** implementation working.

```
<!--script src="scripts/tasks-webstorage.js"></script-->

<script src="scripts/tasks-indexeddb.js"></script>
```

To begin with we are going to implement the **init** method. As with the Web storage implementation, this will check that **IndexedDB** is supported by the browser, but unlike Web Storage, there is a specific operation that needs to be performed: opening the database.

The following is the implementation:

```
storageEngine = function() {

  var database;

    var objectStores;

  return {
```

```
    init : function(successCallback, errorCallback) {
      if (window.indexedDB) {
        var request = indexedDB.open(window.location.hostname+'DB', 1)
        request.onsuccess = function(event) {
          database = request.result;
          successCallback(null);
        }
        request.onerror = function(event) {
          errorCallback('storage_not_initalized',
            'It is not possible to initialized storage');
        }
      } else {
        errorCallback('storage_api_not_supported',
          'The web storage api is not supported');
      }


    },
    initObjectStore : function(type, successCallback, errorCallback) {
    },
    save : function(type, obj, successCallback, errorCallback) {
    },
    findAll : function(type, successCallback, errorCallback) {
    },
    delete : function(type, id, successCallback, errorCallback) {
    },
    findByProperty : function(type, propertyName, propertyValue,
successCallback, errorCallback) {


    },
    findById : function (type, id, successCallback, errorCallback)  {
    }
  }
}();
```

There are a number of things going on here. Firstly, look at this line of code:

```
var request = indexedDB.open(window.location.hostname+'DB')
```

This is the request to open a database. The database may or may not exist before this call. Our implementation is going to create a database named for the domain we are running in, so if we are running using the hostname localhost, the database will be localhostDB, whereas if we are running in the domain www.testing.com, the database will be called www.testing.comDB.

The next point to note is that this returns a synchronous response. The response does not imply the operation has completed however, it is necessary to add **onsuccess** and **onerror** callbacks to the object returned. These will then be fired on success or failure: you can see this occurring on the next few lines.

In the implementation above, the **onsuccess** callback also stores the result of the function call in a private variable called **database**.

If you set a breakpoint and examine the properties of this object you will see the following:

```
request = indexedDB.open(window.location.hostname+'DB', 1
request.onsuccess = function(event) {
    database = request.result;
            ccessCallback(null);
```

```
IDBDatabase
    name: "localhostDB"
  ▶ objectStoreNames: DOMStringList
    onabort: null
    onerror: null
    onversionchange: null
    version: 1
  ▶ __proto__: IDBDatabase
```

This shows that the database has a name and a version, but not much else at this point. The version has been implicitly created for us, but we will see later in this chapter that it is possible to explicitly set this.

Next we will implement the **initObjectStore** method so that the database knows how to store objects of a specific type. Unlike the Web storage API, IndexedDB is going to store our objects directly rather than as serialized strings. IndexedDB can in fact store any data type, including literal strings and numbers, but we are only interested in storing objects.

IndexedDB also relies on the concept of primary keys when storing objects. We can tell IndexedDB the property name that holds the primary key, and we can even ask IndexedDB to generate these for us. In the storage engine the **id** property of the object always represents the primary key.

> In relational databases, all tables typically need a primary key. This can consist of one or more columns, and the value for the primary key must be unique within a table.

The following is the implementation for creating object stores in IndexedDB.

```
initObjectStore  : function(type, successCallback, errorCallback) {
  if (!database) {
    errorCallback( 'storage_api_not_initialized',
      'The storage engine has not been initialized');
  }
  var exists = false;
  $.each(database.objectStoreNames, function(i, v) {
    if (v == type) {
      exists = true;
    }
  });
  if (exists) {
    successCallback(null);
  } else {
    var version = database.version+1;
    database.close();
    var request = indexedDB.open(window.location.hostname+'DB',
      version);
    request.onsuccess = function(event) {
      successCallback(null);
    }
    request.onerror = function(event) {
      errorCallback( 'storage_not_initalized',
        'It is not possible to initialized storage');
    }
    request.onupgradeneeded = function(event) {
      database = event.target.result;
      var objectStore = database.createObjectStore(type,
        {keyPath: "id", autoIncrement: true });
```

```
        }
    }
},
```

The implementation of this method may look difficult to understand. The first portion of this method checks whether the object store for this **type** already exists in the structure of the database:

```
$.each(database.objectStoreNames, function(i, v) {
    if (v == type) {
        exists = true;
    }
});
```

If it does (i.e. this is not the first time the page has been loaded) then we have nothing to do, and the success callback can be invoked.

If we do need to create an object store for this **type** then we are altering the structure of the database. There are very strict rules for changing the structure of the database with IndexedDB, specifically, it can only occur during the process of opening the database.

In order to accommodate this requirement, we need to **close** the database, but before doing that we will also record which version of the database we are using:

```
var version = database.version+1;

database.close();
```

Now, the database can be re-opened, but we will tell IndexedDB that the version number of the database has changed. We could request any version number for the database, but incrementing by one is a natural choice.

```
indexedDB.open(window.location.hostname+'DB', version);
```

Due to the fact that a new version number has been specified, not only will the **onsuccess** and **onerror** functions be invoked on the request, but a third function called **onupgradeneeded** will also be invoked. This function is the only place where we are allowed to change the structure of the database, and we do so with the following call:

```
request.onupgradeneeded = function(event) {
    database = event.target.result;
    var objectStore = database.createObjectStore(type,
        {keyPath: "id", autoIncrement: true });
}
```

On the first line we are re-storing the local reference to the database.

Next we are requesting for an **objectStore** to be created for our **type**. We are also going to specify that the primary key of the object store is contained in the **id** property of persisted objects, and that we want this to be auto incremented by IndexedDB. This means that we no longer need to worry about generating the IDs for objects.

The API we have provided has complicated the object store creation process to some extent. If we knew all the object store names in the **init** method then we would not have needed to close and reopen the database. It has given us more flexibility however, because each functional area of the application can be responsible for initializing itself, without worrying about the rest of the application.

Before proceeding with the code, we need to make a small change to this code in tasks.html:

```
$(document).ready(function() {
    tasksController.init($('#taskPage'));
    tasksController.loadTasks();
});
```

The call to **tasksController.init** will be responsible for initializing the storage engine; therefore it needs to know that it is fully initialized before returning. With the current implementation, the application may start using the storage engine before it is fully initialized, as it would do in the call to **tasksController.loadTasks**.

In order to solve this we are going to make the **init** method in tasks-controller.js use a callback to notify its client when it has truly finished initializing. The following are the changes to the **init** method:

```
init : function(page, callback) {
  if (initialised) {
    callback()
  } else {
    taskPage = page;
    storageEngine.init(function() {
      storageEngine.initObjectStore('task', function() {
        callback();
      }, errorLogger)
    }, errorLogger);
```

The **init** method now accepts a **callback** parameter (which should be a function). If the module is initialized already, it simply invokes the callback by executing the function. If the module is not initialized, the callback is not invoked until the **initObjectStore** method succeeds.

With that in place, we can now change the code in tasks.html as follows:

```
tasksController.init($('#taskPage'), function() {
    tasksController.loadTasks();
});
```

The page will not attempt to load the tasks into its table until the callback has been invoked to notify it that the storage engine has fully initialized.

This is as important lesson to learn: as soon as you start developing asynchronous APIs you need to be conscious of the difference between a function returning control to the caller, and a function finishing processing. It is often not until the function has finished processing that you can perform subsequent actions. It is easy to overlook these situations, and they can be a source of annoying bugs.

The next step in the process is to implement the **save** method. This will introduce you to the concept of IndexedDB transactions:

```
save : function(type, obj, successCallback, errorCallback) {
  if (!database) {
    errorCallback('storage_api_not_initialized',
        'The storage engine has not been initialized');
  }
  if (!obj.id) {
    delete obj.id ;
  } else {
    obj.id = parseInt(obj.id)
  }
  var tx = database.transaction([type], "readwrite");
  tx.oncomplete = function(event) {
    successCallback(obj);
  };
  tx.onerror = function(event) {
    errorCallback('transaction_error',
        'It is not possible to store the object');
  };
  var objectStore = tx.objectStore(type);
  var request = objectStore.put(obj);
  request.onsuccess = function(event) {
    obj.id = event.target.result
  }
  request.onerror = function(event) {
    errorCallback('object_not_stored',
        'It is not possible to store the object');
  };
}
```

After we establish that there is a database to operate on we check the **id** of the object we have been passed. If it is a false value (e.g. null or "") we delete the **id** property itself to make it **undefined**. Since IndexedDB is responsible for generating keys, it does not expect to find an id property at all on an unsaved object, even one with a **null** value. Our implementation of **toObject** will produce empty strings for properties that are empty.

If the property does exist, we ensure that it is an integer with the **parseInt** function. For instance, if we are passed a number as a string, then we convert it to a number. This is another important consideration, since the **toObject** implementation currently always produces strings.

This is the first time we have seen the native JavaScript **parseInt** function. Although this is a useful function, it does have its problems. In order to see these first hand, try the following call:

```
> parseInt(010)
```

It will be left to the reader to discover why this returns 8 rather than 10.

Next we create a transaction in the database and add onerror and onsuccess callbacks to it:

```
var tx = database.transaction([type], "readwrite");
tx.oncomplete = function(event) {
  successCallback(obj);
};
tx.onerror = function(event) {
  errorCallback('transaction_error',
      'It is not possible to store the object');
};
```

We can only access an object store in the context of a transaction. A transaction groups together a set of operations on one or more object stores. The transaction will auto-commit once all requests against the transaction have completed.

It is not until the transaction completes that we will notify the client of success. If we notified the client after the requests had been submitted they might encounter a situation where they cannot query the object store for the objects. This is because all changes to the object store will remain hidden from all clients until the transaction commits.

The transaction is specified as a "readwrite" transaction: you must specify this if you want to modify objects in an object store. The default transaction type is "read". It may seem strange that a transaction is required even to read objects.

Next we perform the request to save an object to the object store.

```
var objectStore = tx.objectStore(type);
var request = objectStore.put(obj);
```

```
request.onsuccess = function(event) {
  obj.id = event.target.result
}
request.onerror = function(event) {
  errorCallback('object_not_stored',
      'It is not possible to store the object');
};
```

Once the object store has been retrieved from the transaction, the **put** method is used to persist the object. This method is capable of supporting updates and inserts. If we only wanted to handle inserts we could have used the **add** method instead.

Just as the transaction has callbacks, the code also adds **onsuccess** and **onerror** callbacks to the **request**. In the **onsuccess** callback we are going to extract the ID that has been assigned to the object so that this can be returned to the client. The **onsuccess** of the request will always be called before the **onsuccess** of the transaction

Next we will implement the **findAll** method. The following is the IndexedDB implementation. This will introduce you to another important IndexedDB concept: cursors. Cursors will be familiar to those of you who have worked with relational databases; a cursor represents a result set, and can be navigated to access all the records in the result set.

```
findAll : function(type, successCallback, errorCallback) {
  if (!database) {
    errorCallback('storage_api_not_initialized',
        'The storage engine has not been initialized');
  }
  var result = [];
  var tx = database.transaction(type);
  var objectStore = tx.objectStore(type);
  objectStore.openCursor().onsuccess = function(event) {
    var cursor = event.target.result;
    if (cursor) {
      result.push(cursor.value);
      cursor.continue();
    } else {
      successCallback(result);
    }
  };
}
```

The initial portion of this should be very familiar. We create a transaction (although we do not specify "readwrite" this time).

```
var tx = database.transaction(type);
var objectStore = tx.objectStore(type);
```

Once we have a transaction we specify the object store we wish to access and open a cursor on it. The **openCursor** method will implicitly create a cursor with all objects in the object store in its result set.

It is also possible to limit the result set returned by **openCursor** to a specific key range.

In order to loop through the contents of the cursor we registered a callback with the **onsuccess** event of the **openCursor** method. This will be called when the cursor is open and ready to be interacted with.

```
objectStore.openCursor().onsuccess = function(event) {
    var cursor = event.target.result;
    if (cursor) {
        result.push(cursor.value);
        cursor.continue();
    } else {
        successCallback(result);
    }
};
```

Within this function we have access to a **cursor** object. If this is **null** then there are no further entries in the result set. If it is not null we can call **cursor.value** to get the object at the current cursor position, and then **cursor.continue** to move the cursor to the next position in the result set.

When the cursor is eventually **null** we know we can return any results we have collected from the cursor to the client. There is no need to wait for the transaction to complete before returning results to the client because the transaction is not modifying the state of the database.

The next method we will implement is **findById**. This will highlight another feature of IndexedDB; it is trivial to access an object with a specific ID inside an object store without the need to loop through all the objects. This is because IndexedDB has an index on the **id** property:

```
findById : function (type, id, successCallback, errorCallback)   {
  if (!database) {
    errorCallback('storage_api_not_initialized',
        'The storage engine has not been initialized');
  }
  var tx = database.transaction([type]);
  var objectStore = tx.objectStore(type);
  var request = objectStore.get(id);
```

```
    request.onsuccess = function(event) {
        successCallback(event.target.result);
    }
    request.onerror = function(event) {
        errorCallback('object_not_stored',
            'It is not possible to locate the requested object');
    };
}
```

This method is very similar to the **findAll** method, except we do not need to open a cursor to find the object we wish to access, instead we can call **get** on the object store and pass in the relevant **id**.

As with all IndexedDB methods, this is still an asynchronous call, therefore we still need to add an event listener to retrieve the object returned. If there is no match for the key, **get** will return a null result, which is also what our storage engine API expects.

The delete implementation is similar to several of the methods we have seen before:

```
delete : function(type, id, successCallback, errorCallback) {
    var obj = {};
    obj.id = id;
    var tx = database.transaction([type], "readwrite");
    tx.oncomplete = function(event) {
        successCallback(id);
    };
    tx.onerror = function(event) {
        console.log(event);
        errorCallback('transaction_error',
            'It is not possible to store the object');
    };
    var objectStore = tx.objectStore(type);
    var request = objectStore.delete(id);
    request.onsuccess = function(event) {
    }
    request.onerror = function(event) {
        errorCallback('object_not_stored',
            'It is not possible to delete the object');
    };
```

}

As with the **save** method, we ensure the transaction is opened with the "readwrite" parameter. We are also careful not to tell the client we have successfully performed the delete until the transaction (rather than the request) completes.

The **delete** method takes advantage of the **delete** method on **objectStore**, which conveniently accepts an ID.

Finally, we will implement the **findByProperty** method. This is one area where you may expect IndexedDB to shine brightest with its ability to query directly for the relevant results rather than looping over all results in JavaScript code.

In fact, IndexedDB can perform queries for properties with specific values, but only if an index has been created on that property. In a situation where any property can form the basis of a query, this would mean adding indexes to all properties on an object.

We will not add an index in our example, but it is worth knowing how they work. In order to create an index, we would need to add the following to the **onupgradeneeded** callback:

```
objectStore.createIndex("category", " category ", { unique: false });
```

Indexes can either be unique or non-unique. The index for the **category** property on the task object would need to be non-unique, since many tasks can have the same **category**.

With that in place we could search for all tasks with a specific category by first obtaining a reference to the index from the object store:

```
var index = objectStore.index("category");
```

Next, you would specify the range you wish to search for (e.g. the index value):

```
var range = IDBKeyRange.only("Work");
```

and then open a cursor on that just as we saw in the **findAll** example, except the range would be passed as a parameter:

```
index.openCursor(range).onsuccess = function(event) {
```

Due to the fact we are not going to add an index to the properties on task, we have no option but to loop through the objects ourselves and determine those that match:

```
findByProperty : function(type, propertyName, propertyValue,
successCallback, errorCallback) {

  if (!database) {

    errorCallback('storage_api_not_initialized',

        'The storage engine has not been initialized');

  }

  var result = [];

  var tx = database.transaction(type);

  var objectStore = tx.objectStore(type);
```

```
    objectStore.openCursor().onsuccess = function(event) {
      var cursor = event.target.result;
      if (cursor) {
        if (cursor.value[propertyName] == propertyValue) {
          result.push(cursor.value);
        }
        cursor.continue();
      } else {
        successCallback(result);
      }
    };
}
```

The complete implementation of the IndexedDB storage engine should now look like this:

```
storageEngine = function() {
  var database;
  var objectStores;
  return {
    init : function(successCallback, errorCallback) {
      if (window.indexedDB) {
        var request = indexedDB.open(window.location.hostname+'DB');
        request.onsuccess = function(event) {
          database = request.result;
          successCallback(null);
        }
        request.onerror = function(event) {
          errorCallback('storage_not_initalized',
            'It is not possible to initialized storage');
        }
      } else {
        errorCallback('storage_api_not_supported',
          'The web storage api is not supported');
      }
    },
    initObjectStore  : function(type, successCallback, errorCallback) {
```

```javascript
        if (!database) {
          errorCallback('storage_api_not_initialized',
              'The storage engine has not been initialized');
        }
        var exists = false;
        $.each(database.objectStoreNames, function(i, v) {
            if (v == type) {
              exists = true;
            }
        });
        if (exists) {
          successCallback(null);
        } else {
          var version = database.version+1;
          database.close();
          var request = indexedDB.open(
              window.location.hostname+'DB', version);
          request.onsuccess = function(event) {
            successCallback(null);
          }
          request.onerror = function(event) {
            errorCallback('storage_not_initalized',
              'It is not possible to initialized storage');
          }
          request.onupgradeneeded = function(event) {
            database = event.target.result;
            var objectStore = database.createObjectStore(type,
              {keyPath: "id", autoIncrement: true });
          }
        }
    },
  save : function(type, obj, successCallback, errorCallback) {
    if (!database) {
      errorCallback('storage_api_not_initialized',
```

```
        'The storage engine has not been initialized');
    }
    if (!obj.id) {
      delete obj.id ;
    } else {
      obj.id = parseInt(obj.id)
    }
    var tx = database.transaction([type], "readwrite");
    tx.oncomplete = function(event) {
      successCallback(obj);
    };
    tx.onerror = function(event) {
      errorCallback('transaction_error',
          'It is not possible to store the object');
    };
    var objectStore = tx.objectStore(type);
    var request = objectStore.put(obj);
    request.onsuccess = function(event) {
      obj.id = event.target.result
    }
    request.onerror = function(event) {
      errorCallback('object_not_stored',
          'It is not possible to store the object');
    };
},
findAll : function(type, successCallback, errorCallback) {
  if (!database) {
    errorCallback('storage_api_not_initialized',
        'The storage engine has not been initialized');
  }
  var result = [];
  var tx = database.transaction(type);
  var objectStore = tx.objectStore(type);
  objectStore.openCursor().onsuccess = function(event) {
```

```javascript
          var cursor = event.target.result;
          if (cursor) {
            result.push(cursor.value);
            cursor.continue();
          } else {
            successCallback(result);
          }
        };
      },
    delete : function(type, id, successCallback, errorCallback) {
      var obj = {};
      obj.id = id;
      var tx = database.transaction([type], "readwrite");
      tx.oncomplete = function(event) {
        successCallback(id);
      };
      tx.onerror = function(event) {
        console.log(event);
        errorCallback('transaction_error',
            'It is not possible to store the object');
      };
      var objectStore = tx.objectStore(type);
      var request = objectStore.delete(id);
      request.onsuccess = function(event) {
      }
      request.onerror = function(event) {
        errorCallback('object_not_stored',
              'It is not possible to delete the object');
      };
    },
    findByProperty : function(type, propertyName, propertyValue,
  successCallback, errorCallback) {
      if (!database) {
        errorCallback('storage_api_not_initialized',
```

```
        'The storage engine has not been initialized');
    }
    var result = [];
    var tx = database.transaction(type);
    var objectStore = tx.objectStore(type);
    objectStore.openCursor().onsuccess = function(event) {
      var cursor = event.target.result;
      if (cursor) {
        if (cursor.value[propertyName] == propertyValue) {
          result.push(cursor.value);
        }
        cursor.continue();
      } else {
        successCallback(result);
      }
    };
  },
  findById : function (type, id, successCallback, errorCallback)  {
    if (!database) {
      errorCallback('storage_api_not_initialized',
          'The storage engine has not been initialized');
    }
    var tx = database.transaction([type]);
    var objectStore = tx.objectStore(type);
    var request = objectStore.get(id);
      request.onsuccess = function(event) {
      successCallback(event.target.result);
    }
    request.onerror = function(event) {
      errorCallback('object_not_stored',
        'It is not possible to locate the requested object');
    };
  }
}
```

```
}();
```

Dynamically Choosing a Storage Engine

We now have two storage engines matching the requirements of our API, they can be used entirely interchangeably (assuming the browser supports the underlying APIs). Our preferred approach is to use the IndexedDB storage engine if it is supported by the browser, and to fallback to the Web storage API if it is not supported.

In order to load the correct storage engine we have two distinct tasks. The first is deciding which storage engine we wish to use; the second is forcing that storage engine to load instead of the other.

In order to determine if it is possible to use a particular storage engine we can use the following:

```
if (window.localStorage) {
```

and

```
if (window.indexedDB) {
```

If the browser supports these APIs there will be a global property on the **window** object for that API, and therefore the **if** statement will evaluate to **true**.

This approach is not foolproof, since there is nothing to stop us creating our own global property called **localStorage** on the **window** object, but it is a quick and convenient mechanism that we can rely on if we are following good coding standards.

Now that we have an approach for determining if a particular storage engine is available, we have several options for loading the correct storage engine at run-time. We will achieve this through the use of AJAX. This will dynamically load the appropriate JavaScript file at run-time based on the capabilities of the browser.

 If you are not familiar with AJAX, you do not need to concern yourself with how it works in this chapter. AJAX will be covered in depth later in the book.

To see how this works, delete both the storage engine imports:

```
<!--script src="scripts/tasks-webstorage.js"></script-->
<script src="scripts/tasks-indexeddb.js"></script>
```

And then replace the following in tasks.html:

```
$(document).ready(function() {
  tasksController.init($('#taskPage'), function() {
    tasksController.loadTasks();
  });
});
```

with this:

```
if (window.indexedDB) {

  $.getScript( "scripts/tasks-indexeddb.js" )

    .done(function( script, textStatus ) {

      $(document).ready(function() {

        tasksController.init($('#taskPage'), function() {

          tasksController.loadTasks();

        });

      })

    })

    .fail(function( jqxhr, settings, exception ) {

        console.log( 'Failed to load indexed db script' );

    });

} else if (window.localStorage) {

    $.getScript( "scripts/tasks-webstorage.js" )

    .done(function( script, textStatus ) {

      $(document).ready(function() {

        tasksController.init($('#taskPage'), function() {

          tasksController.loadTasks();

        });


      })

    })

    .fail(function( jqxhr, settings, exception ) {

        console.log( 'Failed to load web storage script' );

  });

}
```

This is taking advantage of the $.getScript helper in jQuery to load the appropriate JavaScript via an asynchronous AJAX call. The result of the AJAX call is the script we wish to load, which jQuery is then dynamically adding to the DOM.

Due to the fact the JavaScript is now dynamically loading the appropriate storage engine at run-time, we also need to ensure we do not start using the storage engine until the script has been loaded. We therefore initialize the screen inside the success (done) callbacks from the AJAX calls.

The current implementation duplicates the initialization logic for each script we attempt to load; therefore we can rewrite it as follows:

```
function initScreen() {
  $(document).ready(function() {
    tasksController.init($('#taskPage'), function() {
      tasksController.loadTasks();
    });
  });
}
if (window.indexedDB) {
  $.getScript( "scripts/tasks-indexeddb.js" )
  .done(function( script, textStatus ) {
    initScreen();
  })
  .fail(function( jqxhr, settings, exception ) {
    console.log( 'Failed to load indexed db script' );
  });
} else if (window.localStorage) {
  $.getScript( "scripts/tasks-webstorage.js" )
  .done(function( script, textStatus ) {
    initScreen();
  })
  .fail(function( jqxhr, settings, exception ) {
    console.log( 'Failed to load web storage script' );
  });
}
```

An alternative approach we could have followed would be to download both the scripts as traditional imports, but load them in order. We could have then added logic to only create a storage engine if:

1. The browser supports the underlying API.

2. There is no storage engine already created.

We would achieve the same result with this approach. The only disadvantage of this is that we would be loading one extra script that we did not need.

11 TIDYING UP THE WEB APPLICATION

We now have most of the pieces of the application in place, but before continuing there are a number of features we need to add. These features will help to reinforce the knowledge you have already gained in earlier chapters. You may wish to attempt to implement these features on your own based on the short introduction given to each.

Updating the Count

We need to update the count at the bottom of the screen every time there is a change to the number of tasks:

You have 3 tasks

In order to do this, we will change this element:

```
<footer>You have 3 tasks</footer>
```

to this:

```
<footer>You have <span id="taskCount"></span> tasks</footer>
```

Wrapping the number in a span will not alter the presentation, but it allows us to find the element in the DOM, and update it when required.

Now we want to add a function to the tasks-controller.js that counts the number of rows in the table and updates the element appropriately:

```
tasksController = function() {
  function errorLogger(errorCode, errorMessage) {
```

```
        console.log(errorCode +':'+ errorMessage);
    }
    var taskPage;
    var initialised = false;


    function taskCountChanged() {
      var count = $(taskPage).find( '#tblTasks tbody tr').length;
      $('footer').find('#taskCount').text(count);
    }
```

Finally, we want to call this function in the **loadTasks** method:

```
loadTasks : function() {
  storageEngine.findAll('task', function(tasks) {
  $.each(tasks, function(index, task) {
    $('#taskRow').tmpl(task ).appendTo(
        $(taskPage).find('#tblTasks tbody'));
    });
    taskCountChanged();
  }, errorLogger);
}
```

And we also need to call it after deleting a task – since in that case we do not call **loadTasks**:

```
$(taskPage).find('#tblTasks tbody').on('click', '.deleteRow',
  function(evt) {
    storageEngine.delete('task', $(evt.target).data().taskId,
    function() {
      $(evt.target).parents('tr').remove();
      taskCountChanged();
    }, errorLogger);
  });
```

The only thing to note about this implementation is that the **footer** is not part of the tasks page: therefore we cannot access the **footer** in the context of $(taskPage).

Clear Task

Next we want to implement the clear task functionality. This should be invoked when the "Clear

Task" button is clicked, but should also be invoked after a **save**.

There is a very convenient way to implement the clear task functionality. Add the following code to the private section of tasks-controller.js:

```
function clearTask() {
  $(taskPage).find('form').fromObject({});
}
```

We can simply de-serialize an empty object into the form. This will ensure that all form elements have their content cleared, since they will not find a corresponding value in the object passed in.

Now we can add the following to the **init** method of the tasks-controller.js where the other event listeners were registered:

```
$(taskPage).find('#clearTask').click(function(evt) {
  evt.preventDefault();
  clearTask();
});
```

We also want to invoke clear tasks after a save (we added code for this previously, but it is worth changing to utilize the new implementation). Change line of code:

```
$(':input').val('');
```

to the following:

```
clearTask();
```

Overdue tasks

The next feature we will add is functionality to render the background of rows to show tasks that are due in the next 2 days in orange, and tasks that are overdue in a light red color.

Before doing so, you may have noticed that this functionality to highlight rows no longer works:

```
$(taskPage).find('tbody tr').click(function(evt) {
    $(evt.target).closest('td').siblings().andSelf().
      toggleClass('rowHighlight');
});
```

The reason for this should now be obvious: we are adding listeners when the screen loads, but the tasks have not been loaded into the table at this point. We need to change these to be a "live" event listeners using the approach documented in the jQuery chapter:

```
$(taskPage).find('#tblTasks tbody').on('click', 'tr', function(evt) {
    $(evt.target).closest('td').siblings().andSelf().
      toggleClass('rowHighlight');
});
```

Now we are going to add functionality to render the background of the tasks. This will utilize the following classes defined in tasks.css:

```css
.overdue {
    background: #F7DCE5;
}


.warning {
    background: #F7F7DC;
}
```

We have two options for assigning the correct class to rows in the table: we can do it in the template, or we can do it after all rows have been loaded in JavaScript. We will choose the later option.

In order to implement this functionality it is necessary to compare dates in tasks to the current date. JavaScript has a set of rudimentary functions for dealing with dates, but it is usually advisable to use a specialized date library if you need to perform extensive date manipulation or calculations. This application will utilize the following library:

http://www.datejs.com/

 The JavaScript date object was modeled on the Date class in Java. It was such a direct copy that it even included the same bugs related to Y2K. Thankfully these have been resolved long ago.

Download the latest version, add it to the scripts folder, and then import it into the tasks.html page (make sure this is added after jQuery loads – it does not directly use jQuery but redefines a method jQuery relies on):

```html
<script src="scripts/date.js"></script>
```

Now, refresh the tasks.html page in the browser and open the console, you can now use function calls such as this:

```
> Date.today()


> (2).months().ago()


> (3).days().fromNow();
```

As you can see, this is a very intuitive date library, and is far superior to the inbuilt library.

We can now add the following function to tasks-controlller.js immediately after the **clearTasks** function we just added:

```javascript
function renderTable() {
  $.each($(taskPage).find('#tblTasks tbody tr'), function(idx, row) {
```

```
var due = Date.parse($(row).find('[datetime]').text());
if (due.compareTo(Date.today()) < 0) {
  $(row).addClass("overdue");
} else if (due.compareTo((2).days().fromNow()) <= 0) {
  $(row).addClass("warning");
}
});
}
```

This will iterate through all the rows in the table and extract their date from the attribute called **datetime** (you will remember that this conformed to the ISO date standard, therefore it can be parsed directly without having to specify its format).

Once the date has been identified it will be parsed using the date library from a string to a date. We will then compare that date to today: if the result is less than 0 the date is in the past, and we add the **overdue** class.

If the date is not in the past, we see if it is less than or equal to 2 days from now. If so we add the **warning** class.

We could have written JavaScript to perform these operations without importing a date library, but our code would have been less succinct, and open to bugs. The advantage of using a library is that it has undergone testing by everyone who has used it; therefore the level of quality tends to be high.

We now need to invoke this when the table is loaded:

```
loadTasks : function() {
  storageEngine.findAll('task', function(tasks) {
    $.each(tasks, function(index, task) {
      $('#taskRow').tmpl(task).appendTo( $(taskPage).find('#tblTasks tbody'));
    });
    taskCountChanged();
    renderTable();
  }, errorLogger);
}
```

If you now add tasks that are overdue, or due within the next 2 days, they should be rendered appropriately.

Completing tasks

Next we will implement the "Complete task" functionality. If a task is completed we want to render the text with a strike through it. This will be achieved with the following class from tasks.css:

```
.taskCompleted {

    text-decoration: line-through;

}
```

We also need to store the fact that a task has been completed in the task itself, therefore we will add a new property to a completed task called **complete** and set this to **true** when it is completed.

The first step in the process is to change the complete buttons to have a class we can identify, and make the task **id** accessible to them:

```
<script id="taskRow" type="text/x-jQuery-tmpl">

<tr>

  <td>${task}</td>

  <td><time datetime="${requiredBy}"> ${requiredBy}</time></td>

  <td>${category}</td>

  <td>

    <nav>

      <a href="#" class="editRow" data-task-id="${id}">Edit</a>

      <a href="#" class="completeRow" data-task-id="${id}">Complete</a>

      <a href="#" class="deleteRow" data-task-id="${id}">Delete</a>

    </nav>

  </td>

</tr>

</script>
```

Next, add a listener to these buttons. This will find the task that needs to be completed, save it with a completed property set to **true**, and redraw the table:

```
$(taskPage).find('#tblTasks tbody').on('click', '.completeRow',
function(evt) {

  storageEngine.findById('task', $(evt.target).data().taskId,

    function(task) {

      task.complete = true;

      storageEngine.save('task', task, function() {

        tasksController.loadTasks();

    },errorLogger);

  }, errorLogger);

});
```

We will also make a slight change to the loadTasks method in tasks-controller.js to ensure incomplete tasks have the complete property set to false when the table loads:

```
loadTasks : function() {
  $(taskPage).find('#tblTasks tbody').empty();
  storageEngine.findAll('task', function(tasks) {
    $.each(tasks, function(index, task) {
      if (!task.complete) {
        task.complete = false;
      }
      $('#taskRow').tmpl(task).appendTo( $(taskPage).
        find('#tblTasks tbody'));
      taskCountChanged();
      renderTable();
    });
  }, errorLogger);
}
```

The next step is to have the template check for completed tasks. If a task is completed, the **td** elements will be given the class **taskCompleted**, and the complete and edit buttons will not be displayed. This was why we needed to set the completed property on all tasks – the template engine will error if undefined properties are accessed:

```
<script id="taskRow" type="text/x-jQuery-tmpl">
<tr>
    <td {{if complete ==
true}}class="taskCompleted"{{/if}}>${task}</td>
    <td {{if complete == true}}class="taskCompleted"{{/if}}><time
datetime="${requiredBy}">${requiredBy}</time></td>
    <td {{if complete ==
true}}class="taskCompleted"{{/if}}>${category}</td>
    <td>
        <nav>
            {{if complete != true}}
                <a href="#" class="editRow" data-task-
id="${id}">Edit</a>
                <a href="#" class="completeRow" data-task-
id="${id}">Complete</a>
            {{/if}}
            <a href="#" class="deleteRow" data-task-
id="${id}">Delete</a>
        </nav>
```

```
    </td>
  </tr>
</script>
```

This is the first time we have used a conditional construct within a template, and once again, this shows the advantages of using a template engine.

With this in place, you should be able to complete a task and have it appear as follows:

Name	Due	Category	Actions
new task	2013-06-24	Personal	Delete

We can still delete a completed task, but we can no longer edit or complete them.

Sorting tasks

The final change we will make is to sort tasks so that the ones due earliest are sorted first.

We will again use the date library for parsing and comparing dates, but we will use the standard **sort** method available on arrays to perform the sorting.

The **sort** method accepts a comparator as an argument. A comparator is a function that can compare any two elements in an array and determine which ranks higher. A comparator should return a value less than 1 to indicate the first element is higher, 0 if they are equal, or a number greater than 1 if the second element ranks higher. Date objects already have a **compareTo** method that performs this task.

The sort method will compare the relevant items in the array to determine their relative order. This does not mean comparing all items with one another due to the fact it can rely on transitivity:

If A > B and B > C then A > C.

We can add sorting with a single line in the **loadTasks** method:

```
loadTasks : function() {
  $(taskPage).find('#tblTasks tbody').empty();
  storageEngine.findAll('task', function(tasks) {
    tasks.sort(function(o1, o2) {
      return Date.parse(o1.requiredBy).compareTo(
        Date.parse(o2.requiredBy));
    });
    $.each(tasks, function(index, task) {
      if (!task.complete) {
        task.complete = false;
      }
      $('#taskRow').tmpl(task).appendTo( $(taskPage).find('#tblTasks
tbody'));
```

```
      taskCountChanged();

      renderTable();

    });

  }, errorLogger);

}
```

Conclusion

This completes the basic requirements for the tasks web applications. In the next few chapters we will incorporate features from more advanced HTML5 APIs to allow offline storage of the web application, and the use of files in the application.

12 OFFLINE WEB APPLICATIONS

We have now created a web application that is capable of storing its content in the browser, but unlike a traditional desktop application, this application is still dependent on an Internet connection to load the HTML, CSS and JavaScript resources.

If we are running the Web Server locally this is not an issue, since accessing localhost does not rely on an Internet connection, but obviously a real application would be hosted remotely, and it is sometimes desirable to allow the user to continue using the web application even when disconnected from the Internet.

In this chapter we will write functionality to store the application resources on the client so that after the first time the document is loaded, the client is no longer dependent on an Internet connection to serve the web page. This will be achieved through another HTML5 specification called the Application Cache.

The Application Cache specification allows you to specify a set of resources that should be stored on the client. Once these resources are persisted on the client, the client will not attempt to access these resources from the server on future page loads: it will instead use the versions in the client side Application Cache.

This functionality may sound similar to the caching functionality that browsers have natively supported for years. Browsers typically cache any resources that are downloaded, and then use these versions the next time they are requested unless they have changed.

This form of caching is not intended to support offline web pages however, since this caching functionality still relies on an Internet connection to determine whether a resource has changed. The Application Cache specification on the other hand is specifically designed to store resources offline, and only use these versions until requested to retrieve an update.

Before beginning this section, it is worth mentioning that the examples in this chapter will not use CDN based scripts: they will assume all the JavaScript resources required are served from the **scripts** folder. If you have been using CDNs to serve the jQuery resources, you may want to download them instead and add them to the scripts folder so the examples are the same. This is not a requirement of the application cache (provided the NETWORK property is set appropriately: more on this below), but it allows for a consistent set of examples.

In order to implement an Application Cache we will begin by creating a file called tasks.appcache in the same directory as the tasks.html page.

The Application Cache will contain 3 sections, so begin by adding the following skeleton to the newly created file. An empty line must separate the sections from one another.

```
CACHE MANIFEST


FALLBACK:


NETWORK:
```

The first section of the file is where we list all the resources that we wish to store offline. The order the resources are listed is not important (please check the paths are correct for the files you have in your development environment):

```
CACHE MANIFEST

tasks.html

scripts/date.js

scripts/jquery-2.0.3.js

scripts/jquery-serialization.js

scripts/jquery-tmpl.js

scripts/jquery.validate.js

scripts/tasks-controller.js

scripts/tasks-indexeddb.js

scripts/tasks-webstorage.js

styles/tasks.css


FALLBACK:


NETWORK:
```

These paths are all relative to the application cache file, but absolute paths can also be used. It is very important that all the paths are correct, because if even one of the resources is not available, no files will be added to the browser appcache, and the application will not be available offline.

This is part of the Application Cache specification, even though it seems counter intuitive. It is therefore also vitally important that if a resource is removed from the application it is removed from this manifest.

The purpose of the FALLBACK section is to specify alternative versions of a file that should be used while offline. For instance, we may have an image called online.png that is displayed at the top of the screen when we are online, but we want to display an image called offline.png when we are offline. In order to implement this, we would first add offline.png to the list of cached files in the CACHE MANIFEST section; we would then add the following to the FALLBACK section:

```
FALLBACK:
online.png offline.png
```

We will also find an alternative use of this section below.

The final section is the network section. This is a particularly important section, because it specifies the network addresses the browser may access. If we were to enter the following:

```
NETWORK:
/
```

Then the browser would only be able to access resources from the server in question, it would not be able to access any other servers, for instance, Google Analytics, or files served from CDNs.

The most common setting for this section is as follows:

```
NETWORK:
*
```

This ensures the web application has unrestricted access to the Network.

The next version of the file will look like this:

```
CACHE MANIFEST
tasks.html
scripts/date.js
scripts/jquery-2.0.3.js
scripts/jquery-serialization.js
scripts/jquery-tmpl.js
scripts/jquery.validate.js
scripts/tasks-controller.js
scripts/tasks-indexeddb.js
scripts/tasks-webstorage.js
styles/tasks.css

FALLBACK:

NETWORK:
*
```

We now need to tell the tasks.html file to download this manifest when it is loaded, this in turn will cause the browser to download all the files in the manifest whether they are needed immediately or not. In order to do this, we add a new attribute to the **html** tag in tasks.html:

```
<html lang="en" manifest="tasks.appcache">
```

With this added, request the tasks.html page from the web server. You should not notice anything different, since you have connectivity to the web server. If however you navigate to the following URL in Chrome:

```
chrome://appcache-internals/
```

You will see that the application has been cached; along with a summary of the application size, and the date the cache was created, last updated and last accessed:

Manifest: http://localhost:8080/tasks.appcache

Remove View Entries

- Size: 339 kB
- Creation Time: Wednesday, September 18, 2013 11:50:38 AM
- Last Update Time: Wednesday, September 18, 2013 11:50:38 AM
- Last Access Time: Wednesday, September 18, 2013 11:50:38 AM

You can select to view the entries in this cache; this will show you all the files that have been cached offline.

Manifest: http://localhost:8080/tasks.appcache

Remove View Entries

- Size: 339 kB
- Creation Time: Wednesday, September 18, 2013 11:50:38 AM
- Last Update Time: Wednesday, September 18, 2013 11:50:38 AM
- Last Access Time: Wednesday, September 18, 2013 11:53:07 AM

Flags	URL	Size (headers and data)
Explicit,	http://localhost:8080/scripts/date.js	25.4 kB
Explicit,	http://localhost:8080/scripts/jquery-2.0.3.js	237 kB
Explicit,	http://localhost:8080/scripts/jquery-serialization.js	669 B
Explicit,	http://localhost:8080/scripts/jquery-tmpl.js	19.4 kB
Explicit,	http://localhost:8080/scripts/jquery.validate.js	38.3 kB
Explicit,	http://localhost:8080/scripts/tasks-controller.js	3.4 kB
Explicit,	http://localhost:8080/scripts/tasks-indexeddb.js	5.0 kB
Explicit,	http://localhost:8080/scripts/tasks-webstorage.js	4.0 kB
Explicit,	http://localhost:8080/styles/tasks.css	2.1 kB
Manifest,	http://localhost:8080/tasks.appcache	510 B
Master, Explicit,	http://localhost:8080/tasks.html	3.2 kB

If you have the console open while loading the page you should also see it downloading all the resources. This is a good way to troubleshoot if the application cache is failing to cache resources, since it will tell you the resource that is failing:

```
Creating Application Cache with manifest http://localhost:8080/tasks.appcache
Application Cache Checking event
Application Cache Downloading event
Application Cache Progress event (0 of 10) http://localhost:8080/scripts/tasks-controller.js
Application Cache Progress event (1 of 10) http://localhost:8080/tasks.html
Application Cache Progress event (2 of 10) http://localhost:8080/styles/tasks.css
Application Cache Progress event (3 of 10) http://localhost:8080/scripts/jquery-2.0.3.js
Application Cache Progress event (4 of 10) http://localhost:8080/scripts/jquery-serialization.js
Application Cache Progress event (5 of 10) http://localhost:8080/scripts/jquery.validate.js
Application Cache Progress event (6 of 10) http://localhost:8080/scripts/date.js
Application Cache Progress event (7 of 10) http://localhost:8080/scripts/tasks-webstorage.js
Application Cache Progress event (8 of 10) http://localhost:8080/scripts/jquery-tmpl.js
Application Cache Progress event (9 of 10) http://localhost:8080/scripts/tasks-indexeddb.js
Application Cache Progress event (10 of 10)
Application Cache Cached event
```

If you are using localhost for the web server domain you will need to shutdown the web server to simulate offline mode, since even without network connectivity your browser can access the localhost domain.

Unfortunately, if you shutdown the web server and attempt to load the application you will discover that there is a problem loading the application:

```
Document was loaded from Application Cache with manifest http://localhost:8080/tasks.appcache    tasks.html:1
Application Cache Checking event                                                                  tasks.html:1
Application Cache Error event: Manifest fetch failed (-1) http://localhost:8080/tasks.appcache    tasks.html:1
Failed to load indexed db script                                                                  tasks.html:82
Failed to load resource                    http://localhost:8080/scripts/tasks-indexeddb.js?_=1379462056874
>
```

When we attempt to conditionally load files with the jQuery method $.getScript it is appending the current timestamp to the request, this is to stop the browser caching the script. This means that the browser does not realize that it has a cached version of this file, and therefore fails to load.

We could resolve this issue by asking jQuery to suppress this behavior, but we will instead solve the problem with the features available in the Application Cache API.

It may seem that you should be able to resolve this with the use of a wildcard in the FALLBACK section:

FALLBACK:

scripts/tasks-webstorage.js* scripts/tasks-webstorage.js

scripts/tasks-indexeddb.js* scripts/tasks-indexeddb.js

Unfortunately the fallback section does not allow the use of wildcards. Fortunately, the first URL on each line in the FALLBACK does still represent a pattern: any URL that starts with the text in the URL will match the line in the FALLBACK. Therefore you can simply add the following:

FALLBACK:

scripts/tasks-webstorage.js scripts/tasks-webstorage.js

scripts/tasks-indexeddb.js scripts/tasks-indexeddb.js

This will then state that any URL that starts with:

scripts/tasks-webstorage.js

for example:

scripts/tasks-indexeddb.js?_=1379463013652

should use the resource :

scripts/tasks-indexeddb.js

(which has been stored offline).

With this in place you should be able to reload the tasks.html page, which in turn will ensure the revised version of the manifest will be loaded. You should then be able to shutdown the web server, and hit reload, and have the page display. Even if you restart Chrome with the server shutdown, you can still load the tasks.html page.

The final subject we need to address with the Application Cache is how do you reload resources when they are changed? The browser will use the cached versions of files whether it is online or offline, therefore changing any of the resources in the application will not be reflected on the client, even if the client has access to the server.

The browser will download fresh copies of resources only when the manifest file itself changes. This sounds problematic, since you may not have anything you wish to change in the manifest file, yet still wish to load new versions of the resources. The solution to this is to add a comment in the manifest file, and change this comment every time the resources change, for example:

```
# version 1
```

Any line starting with a # is a comment, however changes to comments are sufficient to force the application cache to refresh. We can therefore continue incrementing this version number each time we want the cache to reload the resources.

If you save this change and reload the page, Chrome should inform you that the cache has an "last update time" of now, even though the "creation time" is in the past:

Manifest: http://localhost:8080/tasks.appcache

Remove View Entries

- Size: 339 kB
- Creation Time: Wednesday, September 18, 2013 12:10:08 PM
- Last Update Time: Wednesday, September 18, 2013 12:16:18 PM
- Last Access Time: Wednesday, September 18, 2013 12:16:18 PM

If you have the console open you will also see the resources being downloaded.

Many features of the Application Cache API seem counter-intuitive. A further aspect that may surprise you about the update process is that the user will not see any updated resources the first time they load the page. The way the application cache works is to first present the user with the web page (using the cached version of resources), and then begin updating and storing the new version of the application in the app cache. It is not therefore until the second time the user loads the page that they will see any updated content.

A side effect of this is that the very first time the tasks.html page is loaded the browser will access all resources twice. The first time will be to load all the resources for display to the user; the second time will be to download them for the cache.

If this is a problem, it is possible to listen for application cache events in order to be notified of cases where the browser discovers it needs to download a new version of the application:

```
window.applicationCache.addEventListener('downloading', function(e) {});
```

In order to add a listener that fires as each resource is downloaded you can add the following:

```
window.applicationCache.addEventListener('progress', function(e) {});
```

Finally, to register an event listener to be notified when all resources have finished updating add the following:

```
window.applicationCache.addEventListener(updateready, function(e) {});
```

In this function it would be possible to call the following if you want the client to have immediate access to the revised application:

```
window.location.reload();
```

13 WORKING WITH FILES

When writing desktop applications, the ability to read and write files from the users file-system is taken for granted. Once a client application is installed on a computer, it largely has full access to all the files the user can access.

Web applications running inside a web browser are naturally restricted in how they can access the users file-system. Users would naturally be very nervous if any web site could read files on their file-system.

Since its early days, HTML has supported a file form element that allowed the user to select a file from their file-system, and post its contents to the server. Even this was subject to tight restrictions: it was not possible to interact with this field via JavaScript in any way, including accessing the contents of a file that the user had selected.

HTML5 includes several APIs for interacting with the users file-system. The most ambitious of these is the File System and File Writer APIs. These specifications have been proposed by Google and are currently only supported in Chrome. They allow a web application to read files, create directories and write files in a virtual file-system.

The word "virtual" is the key here. Each origin will be given its own virtual file-system that it has full control over, but this will be partitioned from both the users real file-system, and the file-system of any pages loaded from any other origin. In addition, depending on how the API is implemented, the virtual file-system may not exist as a set of files and directories on the users file-system (it could be implemented as a binary database).

As a result of the other storage options we have examined in earlier chapters, these APIs are of limited use, and you may be advised to continue using the other storage options we have discussed.

The other major file related API is the FileReader API. This is a simpler, but in many ways more interesting API. It relies on the HTML file form field, but once a file is selected it provides the developer access to the file contents in JavaScript. This means it is possible to perform local parsing of a file without ever submitting it to the web server.

This has several advantages:

1. The user can load files when they are offline (provided the web application has been made to

work offline using the other techniques outlined in this book).

2. The contents of a file could be submitted to the server using an AJAX call rather than a server post.

3. The client could choose to send a subset of a file to the server rather than the whole file, therefore reducing bandwidth requirements.

All major web browsers now support the FileReader API.

In order to demonstrate the FileReader API, we are going to allow users to import a set of tasks from a comma separated (CSV) file. The CSV file will contain three columns:

1. Task description.

2. Date required by.

3. Task category.

The CSV file will contain a single row header, and all other lines will contain tasks.

The following is an example CSV file (this is available in the chapter13 zip file from the book's web site):

```
Task,Required By,Category
Prepare slide show,2013-11-20,Work
Attend Product Lanuch,2013-11-21,Work
```

As a first step, we will provide an import option on the main screen. Add the following code immediately before the closing **main** tag in tasks.html:

```
<section id="csvImport">
<div>
        <label for="task">Import tasks from a CSV file</label>
        <input  type="file" id="importFile" name="importFile"/>
    </div>
</section>
```

We will next add a function to tasks-controller.js that will listen for a change event on the file input field, and then read the file contents. Add this in the private section of the tasks-controller.js file:

```
function loadFromCSV(event) {
  var reader = new FileReader();
  reader.onload = function(evt) {
    console.log(evt.target.result);
  };
  reader.onerror = function(evt) {
```

```
    errorLogger('cannot_read_file', 'The file specified cannot be
read');
    };
    reader.readAsText(event.target.files[0]);
}
```

This is going to receive an event when the file is selected. The first thing this function will do is create a new FileReader object. The FileReader is asked to read the file specified, and then makes the contents available asynchronously, so we also need to add listeners for success and failure. The **onload** listener will be called with the file contents; the **onerror** will be called after any failure.

It is possible for the user to select multiple files at the same time; therefore the target of the event will refer to an array of files. In our case we will ignore the fact this is an array and simply choose the first file:

```
event.target.files[0]
```

Now add the following code in the **init** method of tasks-controller.js to listen for the user selecting a file:

```
$('#importFile').change(loadFromCSV);
```

Once the listener has been added, try loading the file using the file chooser. (The code will simply log the contents of the file for now).

If you examine the target of the event in the debugger you will see it makes information available about the file, including its name, type and modified date:

```
> file.target.files[0]
  ▼ File {webkitRelativePath: "", lastModifiedDate: Sat Sep 21 20.
    ▶ lastModifiedDate: Sat Sep 21 2013 14:59:31 GMT+1200 (NZST)
      name: "test.csv"
      size: 99
      type: "text/csv"
      webkitRelativePath: ""
    ▶ __proto__: File
```

Determining the type of a file that has been loaded can be important, since the FileReader makes available a number of different mechanisms for reading different types of file. In our case we have used **readAsText**, which makes the file contents available as a JavaScript string, but the FileReader also supports the following:

• **readAsBinaryString**: The file contents is made available as a string, but each byte is represented by a number. If the data is textual this will be identical to readAsText.

• **readAsDataURL**: The file contents is made available as an encoded URL. If we load a text document, the contents will be encoded in Base 64 encoding.

• **readAsArrayBuffer**: This can be used if you wish to access a specific part of a file.

Now that we have an event handler that is capable of extracting the contents of the file as a string, the next step is to break this down into an array of lines: this will allow us to process the lines one at a time. We use the split method supported by JavaScript strings to split the string each time it encounters a new line character. This returns an array of strings.

```
function loadFromCSV(event) {
  var reader = new FileReader();
  reader.onload = function(evt) {
    var contents = evt.target.result;
    var lines = contents.split('\n');
  };
  reader.onerror = function(evt) {
    errorLogger('cannot_read_file',
      'The file specified cannot be read');
  };
  reader.readAsText(event.target.files[0]);
}
```

Once we have an array of lines we need to break each line down into a set of tokens, each of which we know is separated by a comma. This may sound relatively simple, for instance the following implementation would meet most of our needs:

```
line.split(',')
```

Unfortunately, CSV files can be more complex than the simple example we have used. For instance, individual tokens may contain commas; therefore a CSV file can wrap a token inside double quotes to ensure that these commas are treated literally rather than as token separators.

Whenever you encounter a problem that looks common (such as parsing a line in a CSV file) it is worth looking for libraries that have already been written. The authors of these libraries will have thought about most issues that may arise, and any library with a large number of users is likely to have been tested in a large number of scenarios, and therefore should prove more stable.

In this scenario we will use this library:

https://code.google.com/p/jquery-csv/

Download the latest version and add it to the scripts folder of the application. I am using version 0.71.

Next, remember to include the import in the page at the end of the head section of tasks.htmk, and also remember to add a reference to the file in tasks.appcache, since we want this library to be available offline.

```
<script src="scripts/jquery.csv-0.71.js"></script>
```

You can check you have installed the script correctly by executing the following call in the console and checking an object is returned:

```
$.csv
```

We can now write code to parse and create tasks:

```javascript
function loadTask(csvTask) {
  var tokens = $.csv.toArray(csvTask);
  if (tokens.length == 3) {
    var task = {};
    task.task = tokens[0];
    task.requiredBy = tokens[1];
    task.category = tokens[2];
    return task;
  }
  return null;
}


function loadFromCSV(event) {
  var reader = new FileReader();
  reader.onload = function(evt) {
    var contents = evt.target.result;
    var lines = contents.split('\n');
    var tasks = [];
    $.each(lines, function(indx, val) {
      if (indx >= 1 && val) {
        var task = loadTask(val);
        if (task) {
          tasks.push(task);
        }
      }
    });
  };
  reader.onerror = function(evt) {
    errorLogger('cannot_read_file',
        'The file specified cannot be read');
  };
  reader.readAsText(event.target.files[0]);
}
```

After we read each line from the CSV, we send it to another function called **loadTask** which tokenizes it using the CSV library, and constructs a task.

Notice also that we skip the first line in the file (since it is the header line), along with any empty lines by using the following code:

```
if (indx >= 1 && val) {
```

We now have an array of tasks that we wish to save. At this point it may be worth adding another method to our storage engines that performs a **saveAll** operation. This would mean we can leverage transaction support in the underlying storage API (if available) to make sure either all the tasks are persisted or none are. The **saveAll** method will return all the objects saved in the transaction.

The following is the **saveAll** implementation in tasks-webstorage.js (it does not provide transaction support):

```
saveAll : function(type, objs, successCallback, errorCallback) {
  if (!initialized) {
    errorCallback('storage_api_not_initialized',
        'The storage engine has not been initialized');
  } else if (!initializedTables[type]) {
    errorCallback('table_not_initialized',
        'The table '+type+' has not been initialized');
  }
  var storageItem = getStorageObject(type);
  $.each(objs, function(indx, obj) {
    if (!obj.id) {
      obj.id = $.now();
    }
    storageItem[obj.id] = obj;
    localStorage.setItem(type, JSON.stringify(storageItem));
  });
  successCallback(objs);
}
```

And the following is the implementation in tasks-indexeddb.js:

```
saveAll : function(type, objs, successCallback, errorCallback) {
  if (!database) {
    errorCallback('storage_api_not_initialized',
        'The storage engine has not been initialized');
  }
```

```javascript
var tx = database.transaction([type], "readwrite");
tx.oncomplete = function(event) {
  successCallback(objs);
};
tx.onerror = function(event) {
  errorCallback('transaction_error',
      'It is not possible to store the object');
};
var objectStore = tx.objectStore(type);
$.each(objs, function(indx, obj) {
  if (!obj.id) {
    delete obj.id ;
  } else {
    obj.id = parseInt(obj.id)
  }
  var request = objectStore.put(obj);
  request.onsuccess = function(event) {
    obj.id = event.target.result
  }
  request.onerror = function(event) {
    errorCallback('object_not_stored',
        'It is not possible to store the object');
  };
});
}
```

Notice that we only create one transaction and then add multiple requests to it: one for each task. It is not until all these requests complete that the transaction is considered complete, and the client is notified of the success.

Finally, we will add the call to **saveAll** in our code:

```javascript
function loadFromCSV(event) {
  var reader = new FileReader();
  reader.onload = function(evt) {
    var contents = evt.target.result;
    var lines = contents.split('\n');
```

```
  var tasks = [];
  $.each(lines, function(indx, val) {
    if (indx >= 1 && val) {
      var task = loadTask(val);
      if (task) {
        tasks.push(task);
      }
    }
  });
  storageEngine.saveAll('task', tasks, function() {
    tasksController.loadTasks();
  },errorLogger);
  };
  reader.onerror = function(evt) {
    errorLogger('cannot_read_file', 'The file specified cannot be
read');
  };
  reader.readAsText(event.target.files[0]);
}
```

With this in place, you should be able to load a CSV file and have the contents immediately reflected in the tasks table. In addition; it is also possible to use this functionality without connectivity to a web server, since all the processing is occurring entirely on the client.

14 WEB WORKERS

Earlier in this book we discussed how JavaScript utilizes a single thread to perform all processing, and that this is the same thread the browser uses to render the web page. Although there are rudimentary ways of controlling when a piece of code executes using **setTimeout**, there is no way to execute JavaScript on a separate thread, or in multiple threads concurrently.

Most modern computers, and even most smart phones, are capable of executing multiple threads concurrently, since most devices now contain multiple processors or multiple cores. In addition, most software engineers expect multithreading libraries to be built into modern languages.

There are very good reasons why JavaScript is limited to a single thread, for instance, to prevent multiple threads attempted to update the same portion of the Document Object Model simultaneously. There is however a lot of other computation where there would be no issue with multiple threads executing simultaneously.

As an example, consider the CSV file that was processed in the previous chapter. The process of converting a JavaScript string into a set of objects is a self-contained operation, and has no bearing on the DOM (at least until we refreshed the table at the end of the processing). It should therefore be theoretically possible to execute this processing on a separate thread, and only revert back to the main browser thread when we need to update the HTML table.

HTML5 contains an API called Web Workers that allow some degree of multi-threading in HTML applications. This chapter will introduce the Web Worker API, and examine some use-cases where it may be appropriate.

A Web Worker is a block of code in its own JavaScript file. The Web Worker typically listens for messages to be posted to it from the main browser thread. When it receives messages, it performs whatever computation is required of it, but the big difference is that the browser will execute this computation on a separate thread, and therefore if the underlying hardware supports it, this processing can happen concurrently with processing on the main browser thread.

When the Web Worker has finished its processing it can post a message back to the main browser thread, which will perform whatever it needs to with this result, such as updating the DOM.

Before looking at what Web Workers can do, we will first look at their restrictions. Web

Workers do not have access to any of the following objects:

- The window object
- The Document Object Model
- The localstorage object
- The document object

Web Workers can however invoke AJAX calls, and they do have access to all the JavaScript features we examined in the JavaScript section of this book.

As a result of their restrictions, the use-cases for Web Workers is limited. There are however a number of cases where they are relevant. If we envisage a word processing application inside a web browser, there are a number of activities we may want to perform on a regular basis in the background, these might include:

1. Checking which words in the document are misspelt.

2. Checking the grammar of the document against a set of rules.

3. Checking where the page breaks should be placed in the document.

4. Collecting statistics for the number of words and pages in the document.

All of the processing associated with these activities could be done in a Web Worker. The Web Worker could be posted the word processor document on a regular basis, it could perform these potentially intensive activities, and then the results could be posted back to the main thread so that the DOM could be updated to reflect the results.

If all these activities were performed on the main browser thread it is likely that the user would experience lags and delays every time these activities were performed, and as the document increased in size it is likely that these lags would become worse.

We are going to implement a Web Worker that is posted a JavaScript string representing a CSV version of a set of tasks. It is then going to process these and post back an array of tasks.

The first step in this process is the creation of a new JavaScript file for the Web Worker: the code cannot exist in the same JavaScript file as any other code, and each Web Worker must have its own JavaScript file. Create a new file in the scripts folder called tasks-csvparser.js.

The following is the basic structure of our Web Worker:

```
self.addEventListener('message', function(msg) {
    var data = msg.data;
    self.postMessage(null);
}, false);
```

It uses a reference to the **self** object in order to add an event listener that listens for messages. When a message is received, the function passed in the second argument will be invoked (along with the message). The third parameter specifies whether the event needs to be captured or not, if in doubt use **false**.

We will now move the relevant code from tasks-controller.js to the Web Worker:

```javascript
self.addEventListener('message', function(msg) {
  var data = msg.data;
  var lines = data.split('\n');
  var tasks = [];
  jQuery.each(lines, function(indx, val) {
    if (indx >= 1 && val) {
      var task = loadTask(val);
      if (task) {
        tasks.push(task);
      }
    }
  });
  self.postMessage(tasks);
}, false);


function loadTask(csvTask) {
  var tokens = $.csv.toArray(csvTask);
  if (tokens.length == 3) {
    var task = {};
    task.task = tokens[0];
    task.requiredBy = tokens[1];
    task.category = tokens[2];
    return task;
  }
  return null;
}
```

Unfortunately we immediately have a problem: there are two references in this code to the jQuery function "$". This object is registered on the **window** object, and therefore is not accessible from the Web Worker.

The first of these (the $.each) can easily be replaced with a for loop:

```javascript
for (var indx = 0; indx < lines.length; indx++) {
  var val = lines[indx];
  if (indx >= 1 && val) {
    var task = loadTask(val);
```

```
    if (task) {
      tasks.push(task);
    }
  }
};
```

Unfortunately we are stuck when it comes to the use of the csv function:

```
$.csv.toArray(csvTask);
```

It is not even possible to pass the jQuery object into the Web Worker. Ultimately we would have no choice but to find a different library for parsing CSV files.

Although this would not be a problem, it is not the subject of this chapter, so we will simply replace that line with simplified code for splitting the line each time a comma is encountered. As discussed above, there are many real world issues with this code:

```
function loadTask(csvTask) {
  var tokens = csvTask.split(',');
  if (tokens.length == 3) {
    var task = {};
    task.task = tokens[0];
    task.requiredBy = tokens[1];
    task.category = tokens[2];
    return task;
  }
  return null;
}
```

The JavaScript file containing the Web Worker does not need to be explicitly imported in tasks.html. Because we want the worker to be available offline however, we do need to add it to tasks.appcache. This will ensure the Web Worker is stored on the client rather than read from the server on demand when the Web Worker is created.

You will notice that when the Web Worker finishes it posts back an array of task objects to a listener. Now we need to write the code that initializes the Web Worker, posts a message to it, and listens for a message in response. This is the code that will execute on the main browser thread.

In order to instantiate a Web Worker we use the following code:

```
var worker = new Worker('scripts/tasks-csvparser.js');
```

Note that this contains the URL of the JavaScript file that will constitute the Web Worker.

Once the Web Worker is created we need to add an event listener to it so that we can hear when it posts messages back to the main browser thread. In our case, this event listener will receive an array of tasks, which it will then save:

```javascript
worker.addEventListener('message', function(e) {
  var tasks = e.data;
  storageEngine.saveAll('task', tasks, function() {
  tasksController.loadTasks();
  },errorLogger);
}, false);
```

Finally we need to post a message to the Web Worker:

```javascript
worker.postMessage(contents);
```

If we put all of that together, the loadFromCSV function should now look like this:

```javascript
function loadFromCSV(event) {
  var reader = new FileReader();
  reader.onload = function(evt) {
    var contents = evt.target.result;
    var worker = new Worker('scripts/tasks-csvparser.js');
    worker.addEventListener('message', function(e) {
      var tasks = e.data;
      storageEngine.saveAll('task', tasks, function() {
        tasksController.loadTasks();
      },errorLogger);
    }, false);
    worker.postMessage(contents);
  };
  reader.onerror = function(evt) {
    errorLogger('cannot_read_file',
        'The file specified cannot be read');
  };
  reader.readAsText(event.target.files[0]);
}
```

If you execute the load from CSV functionality now you will not notice anything different (unless you loaded an enormous file). Despite that, the parsing of the CSV file is now occurring on a background thread rather than the main browser thread.

The Web Worker will remain open even after it has processed our message, and would accept additional messages if we were to send them. The Web Worker can close itself with a call to:

```javascript
self.close()
```

Or in our case the Web Worker will close when the **loadFromCSV** function ends, and the worker variable falls out of scope.

Accessing browser functionality

The only main browser object a Web Worker object has access to is the **navigator** object. This object can be used to obtain information about the browser, such as the browser vendor and version.

Due to the fact Web Workers are executing in a different environment from the main browser thread they do not have access to the objects or functions created by any imported scripts. Web Workers can however load additional JavaScript files if they require. This can be done with the following function call:

```
importScripts('foo.js');
```

Shared vs Dedicated Web Workers

The Web Workers we have been using up until this point are called Dedicated Web Workers. The only script file that is allowed to post messages to the Web Worker is the one that loaded it. A Shared Web Worker on the other hand can be interacted with from any script that is loaded from the same origin. This may save on operating system resources if you need to access a web worker from multiple script files.

Shared Web Workers are not supported by all browsers that currently support Web Workers, therefore it is worth checking browser support before implementing Shared Web Workers.

Shared Web Workers are instantiated in a similar way to dedicated Web Workers, except the class name is different:

```
var worker = new SharedWorker('scripts/tasks-csvparser.js');
```

The client interaction with Shared Web Workers is also similar to Dedicated Web Workers, except there is an additional abstraction of a port. Event listeners are added to ports:

```
worker.port.addEventListener
```

and messages are posted to ports

```
worker.port.postMessage
```

In addition, a port must be explicitly opened before any messages are posted to it:

```
worker.port.start();
```

Finally, the implementation of the Web Worker itself needs to take into account the different ports. The following is a skeleton for the implementation:

```
self.addEventListener("connect", function (e) {
    var port = e.ports[0];
    port.addEventListener("message", function (e) {
        var data = e.data;
        port.postMessage(data);
```

```
    }, false);
    port.start();
}, false);
```

Notice that the first event listener we are creating allows general connections to the Web Worker. When a connection is received for a new port, we then add a separate event listener for this port, and start the port.

The idea behind Shared Web Workers is that they expose a service to your application, just as an application server might expose a service. Multiple clients can then interact with this service, and their messages will be kept separate.

Conclusion

Web Workers offer interesting potentials to Web Applications: the key is finding the appropriate use-cases.

The most viable use-cases are scenarios where the foreground thread can continue to be utilized while additional code is executed on the background thread. The foreground thread may be doing something as trivial as updating a progress bar for the user: but the benefit of Web Workers is that they will not prevent this happening since they are not monopolizing the foreground thread.

The other main use-case for Web Workers is algorithms that can naturally be multi-threaded. In these cases we can spawn multiple Web Workers, and have each of them complete a portion of the algorithm. On devices with multiple cores or processors this is likely to lead to improved performance. For instance, on a device with 4 cores, a single thread can use at most 25% of the processing power. If 4 Web Workers were spawned we could theoretically use 100% of the processing power, and complete the operation 4 times quicker.

15 AJAX

The web application we have written in this book is largely independent of its web server. The web server is responsible for serving resources, and providing an origin for APIs that implement single-origin policies, but beyond that it is not playing any meaningful role, and in fact, once the application is loaded it can exist independent of the web server.

Most real world web applications need to send or receive data to a web server at some point in their lifecycles. For instance, users may wish to synchronize their task list between multiple devices.

There are two ways a web application can interact with a web server. The most common approach is to perform HTTP POST or GET to the server, and load the HTTP response into the browser.

An HTTP GET request is the most common type of request, and occurs when a page is requested in the browser address bar, or the user clicks on a hyperlink. A GET request specifies a specific resource, but it can also pass data to the server using name/value pairs encoded in the URL, for instance:

http://localhost/viewprofile?username=dane

This GET request contains a single parameter (username); which has been set to a value ("dane").

In order to send larger quantities of data to the server POST requests are generally used. A POST request serializes the data in an HTTP form as a set of key/value pairs. The name of each input field becomes a key, while the current value of the input field becomes the value.

A side effect of traditional HTTP GET and POST requests is that a new web page is loaded as a result (the HTTP response). Even if the URL does not change, and there is only a change to a minor part of the page, there will be a lag as the HTTP request is sent and the response is received and rendered.

A second limitation of traditional HTTP GET and POST requests is that they are synchronous. It is not possible to continue using the web application while the request is in progress: the user must wait for the response to be received and updated in the browser.

If you consider the web application we have developed, a traditional web site would cause a page refresh when the user selects to edit a task. A GET request would be sent to the server, perhaps:

http://localhost/tasks.html?edit=122

And the response would contain the tasks.html page, with the edit section populated. To the user it would look like all the page content disappeared and then reappeared a second or two later.

The alternative approach is AJAX (Asynchronous JavaScript and XML).

AJAX started life as an approach rather than a standard. In 1998 Microsoft implemented a component called XMLHTTP. This allowed content to be dynamically requested from the server and incorporated into the current page without a page refresh. This functionality was later adopted by other web browsers as the XMLHttpRequest object. The XMLHttpRequest is currently undergoing a standardization process and is considered part of HTML5.

The XMLHttpRequest object allows a web page to send HTTP POST and GET requests to the server, and receive data in response, but without refreshing the entire web page. For instance, the request may return a fragment of the page that is then dynamically added to the DOM.

It is worth examing the key aspects of AJAX:

• **Asynchonous**: AJAX requests are asynchronous because the main browser thread does not block while the request is in flight. Responses to requests are handled with callbacks. This means the user does not need to be aware that a request is in flight, and they can continue using the web application as though nothing was happening.

• **JavaScript**: The requests are performed using JavaScript objects, and the response is made available as a JavaScript object.

• **XML**: Originally XMLHttpRequest utilized XML as the data exchange format. In fact, XMLHttpRequest allows any data format to be used, and is now commonly used with JSON rather than XML. It is also common to return HTML from an AJAX call, therefore allowing it to be inserted directly into the DOM.

> In fact, XMLHttpRequest is not dependent on HTTP either; it is supported with other protocols such as FTP. In many respects XMLHttpRequest is the worst named object in the history of JavaScript.

Essentially AJAX is a mechanism for asynchronously sending and/or receiving data from a web server using JavaScript, without a page refresh.

It is possible to perform AJAX calls using the inbuilt JavaScript object, however jQuery provides an AJAX wrapper that provides a more convenient mechanism for performing AJAX calls.

In order to try out some AJAX examples, we will make our server return static JSON when a particular URL is requested.

Create a new directory in the directory containing tasks.html called "server".

Add a file to this called tasks.json, and add the following content:

```
[{"id":100,"task":"first task","requiredBy":"2013-09-
03","category":"Personal"},
```

```
{"id":101,"task":"second task","requiredBy":"2013-10-
03","category":"Work"},

{"id":102,"task":"third task","requiredBy":"2013-09-
05","category":"Work"},

{"id":103,"task":"last task","requiredBy":"2013-09-
08","category":"Personal"}]
```

This JSON contains an array, which in turn contains 4 task objects. Each of these task objects have the same properties as those created by the web application.

In order to request this using AJAX, first browse to the tasks.html page. AJAX calls can only be made to the same server name and port as the page that has been loaded in the browser: this is known as the same-origin policy. There are ways around the same-origin policy if necessary, but these tend to rely on hacks: JSONP is the most prominent approach for this if you are interested.

Next open up the console, and type the following:

```
$.ajax({
  type : "GET",
  dataType: "json",
  url : "/server/tasks.json",
  cache : false,
  success : function(data) {
   console.log(data);
  }
});
```

This request is taking advantage of the jQuery static function $.ajax. Although this is relatively simple, there is quite a lot here that needs explaining:

• The request is an HTTP GET request: this is the default so could have been omitted.

• We specify that the data type returned will be **json**. This is used by jQuery to determine how to parse the result. jQuery does a good job guessing this if it is omitted, so it is not generally necessary to specify it. Other accepted values are xml, script, or html.

• Next we specify the URL of the resource we are accessing: this can be an absolute URL, as shown here, or a relative URL. This does not specify the host and port of the server, since the single-origin policy specifies that this must be the host and port of the document loaded into the browser.

• We indicate that we do not want the browser to cache the result. jQuery will ensure the resource is not cached by appending the current timestamp to the request, exactly as we saw earlier when dynamically loading JavaScript scripts. This is a useful feature, since it is generally not desirable to cache requests for data.

• A callback is provided for success scenarios. This will be called asynchronously when the HTTP response is received, and passed the data received from the request.

jQuery offers a set of shorthand methods that reduce the code required still further. We have already come across these for requesting JavaScript scripts from the server. For instance, the example above could be written as follows:

```
$.getJSON( "/server/tasks.json", function( data ) {
    console.log(data);
});
```

Due to the fact we are using the JSON data format, the data object passed to the callback function will be a JavaScript object, automatically de-serialized from the data received. In this case the object is an array containing four task objects. There is therefore no need to transform the result into a format applicable to our application.

Before continuing, it is worth noting that as of jQuery 1.5 there is a better way to register callbacks using a technique called "promises".

The call to $.ajax actually synchronously returns a type of object called a "promise". Any asynchronous (or potentially asynchronous) API can utilize jQuery promises, and they are widely used both within jQuery and beyond.

If you inspect this object in the debugger it looks like this:

```
▼ Object {readyState: 4, getResponseHeader: function, getAllResponseHeaders: function, setR
  ▶ abort: function ( statusText ) {
  ▶ always: function () {
  ▶ complete: function () {
  ▶ done: function () {
  ▶ error: function () {
  ▶ fail: function () {
  ▶ getAllResponseHeaders: function () {
  ▶ getResponseHeader: function ( key ) {
  ▶ overrideMimeType: function ( type ) {
  ▶ pipe: function ( /* fnDone, fnFail, fnProgress */ ) {
  ▶ progress: function () {
  ▶ promise: function ( obj ) {
    readyState: 4
  ▶ responseJSON: Array[4]
    responseText: "[{"id":100,"task":"first task","requiredBy":"2013-09-03","category":"Pers
  ▶ setRequestHeader: function ( name, value ) {
  ▶ state: function () {
    status: 200
  ▶ statusCode: function ( map ) {
    statusText: "OK"
  ▶ success: function () {
  ▶ then: function ( /* fnDone, fnFail, fnProgress */ ) {
```

A promise has a lifecycle. At any point in time it may be in one of three states: "unfulfilled", "fulfilled" or "failed". The promise may only move from "unfulfilled" to "fulfilled", or "unfulfilled" to "failed". Once a promise has been "fulfilled" or "failed", its value cannot not be changed.

The following code shows the same example written to work with promises.

```
promise = $.ajax({
    type : "GET",
```

```
    url : "/server/tasks.json",
    cache : false
});
promise.done(function(data) {
    console.log(data);
});
promise.fail(function() {
    console.log('A failure occurred');
});
```

When the promise is initially created it has a state of "unfulfilled". Once the response is successfully received, the promise is set to "fulfilled", and the relevant callback ("done") is invoked. If an error occurred, the promised would be set to the state of "failed", and the relevant callback would be invoked ("fail").

There are several advantages to using promises over traditional callbacks, both in this AJAX example, and in your own libraries. The first is that it is possible to add multiple success or failure callbacks:

```
promise = $.ajax({
    type : "GET",
    url : "/server/tasks.json",
    cache : false
});
promise.done(function(data) {
    console.log(data);
});
promise.done(function(data) {
    console.log('Also do this');
});
promise.fail(function() {
    console.log('A failure occurred');
});
```

Secondly, even after the AJAX call has finished, you can still call **done** and **fail** to register callbacks, and these will be executed immediately. This may not sound useful, but consider a case where we do not know if a call will be synchronous or asynchronous.

This may happen in cases where we are caching data on the client: if the data is cached it will be available synchronously, otherwise it will be available asynchronously. This means that when we add a callback, the result may be available immediately, and the promise will actually have been fulfilled when we register our callback. An example of this will be provided below.

The third major benefit of promises is that it is possible to delay a callback until multiple promises have completed. This may be useful if you need to perform multiple AJAX calls, aggregate the data, and update the DOM:

```
promise1 = $.ajax({
  url : "/server/tasks.json",
});
promise2= $.ajax({
  url : "/server/tasks.json",
});
$.when(promise1, promise2).done(function(data1, data2) {
  console.log(data1[0]);
  console.log(data2[0]);
  console.log("Both requests have completed");
});
promise.fail(function() {
  console.log('A failure occurred');
});
```

The great news about promises is that you can use them yourself in your own code APIs. Let's consider a function that performs the caching scenario described above:

```
cachedTasks = function() {
  var tasks = null;
  return {
    getTasks : function() {
      var deferred = $.Deferred();
      if (tasks) {
        deferred.resolve(tasks);
        return deferred.promise();
      } else {
        var promise1 = $.ajax({
          url : "/server/tasks.json",
        });
        promise1.done(function(data) {
          tasks = data;
```

```
        setTimeout(function() {deferred.resolve(tasks)}, 5000);

      })
      return deferred.promise();

    }

  }

}
}();
```

This function is using a closure to hold the cached version of the tasks in a variable called **tasks**. If this is not null, then the tasks have already been cached, and are available for clients. If **tasks** is null an AJAX call is required to retrieve the tasks: this will both populate the cache and return the tasks.

You can see that in either case a promise is being synchronously returned from an instance of $.Deferred() to the client. You can also see that in both cases, this object is set to resolved when the result is available for the client. This call automatically moves the promise into the "fulfilled" state, and ensures any callbacks registered with **done** are invoked.

You will also see that this promise is relying on the promise returned from the $.ajax call in the case where the server is invoked. To help you see the result easier, this code also has added a 5 second delay in cases where we are performing an AJAX call.

In order to get the tasks, we invoke the getTasks method on this module. Just as with the AJAX calls, we add a callback to the promise returned by getTasks:

```
promise = cachedTasks.getTasks();

promise.done(function(data) {

  console.log('I have finished')

});
```

If you execute this you should see the console print out "I have finished" after roughly 5 seconds.

Now, run the exact same code again. You should see "I have finished" printed immediately to the console, since this will use the cached version of the tasks, and therefore the result will be available as soon as the callback is registered with the **done** method.

If you trace the code through you will see that the promise is actually already fulfilled when we call the **done** method to add our callback, and therefore our callback is executed immediately. In fact, even after the callback is executed, it is possible to add a second callback to the promise:

```
promise.done(function(data) {

  console.log('I have finished again')

});
```

This will execute immediately, since the promise is already fulfilled.

The use of promises adds an extra dimension to callback-based programming. When writing asynchronously libraries from scratch it is highly recommended to consider basing them on promises.

We will now return to AJAX. So far we have examined AJAX GET requests. It is also possible to perform HTTP POSTs with AJAX. The most common use of this is to POST the contents of a form to a server, but POST is flexible enough to allow any data structure to be posted.

It is often more convenient to post structured data rather than raw form data. This is because the server components will often be capable of de-serializing structured data (such as JSON or XML) into a rich hierarchy of objects, whereas form data consists of name/value pairs.

The following is an example of a function that sends a task object to the server, and returns a promise to the caller:

```
function sendTask(task) {

  return $.ajax({

        type : "POST",

        url : "/submittask",

        contentType : "application/json",

        data : JSON.stringify(task)

  })

}
```

You will notice that we have set the content type to **application/json**. The default content type is **application/x-www-form-urlencoded**, which is the appropriate content type for an HTML form submission.

It is actually possible to simplify this code significantly with one of jQuery's shorthand methods:

```
return $.post( "/submittask", task );
```

jQuery will infer the appropriate options, and implicitly stringify the task object provided.

There are a number of other options that can be provided when using the $.ajax() method. Most of these are not required in most scenarios, but the following are worth knowing about:

• **async**: AJAX calls do not have to be asynchronous (despite the "A" in AJAX). It is possible to perform synchronous AJAX calls by setting **async** to **false**. This is not recommended without a very good reason however, since the main browser thread will block until the response is received.

• **beforeSend**: This is a pre-request callback that allows you to modify the request before it is sent, for instance, adding specific headers to the request.

• **timeout**: Sets the timeout in milliseconds for AJAX calls. This ensures that calls that do not return in a reasonable amount of time will generate an error to the error callback.

16 SERVER SENT EVENTS AND WEB SOCKETS

AJAX has been an enormously important technique in allowing the creation of rich and dynamic web applications. It is worth pausing to consider however that AJAX is still using the same basic underlying communication protocol that has been used since the beginning of the World Wide Web: the client (the web browser) sends an HTTP request to the server (a web server). The web server responds with a synchronous HTTP response. Once the response is received the communication is considered complete.

Although this technique works well enough in most scenarios, it is not well suited to two key scenarios:

1. The server wishes to push information to the client. For instance the server may have a notification that needs to be sent to the client.

2. The client and server wish to hold a long running conversation with many small messages transferred back and forth. For instance, consider a real time multi-player game: data must be transferred back and forward to each client on a regular basis as each user performs activities that affect the other users.

Although both of these use-cases can be supported by HTTP, HTTP is not the optimal protocol for either of these scenarios, due both to its overheads, and its stateless nature. In this chapter we will look at the problems HTTP has adapting to these use-cases, and the solutions offered by HTML5.

Before continuing however, it is worth noting that the APIs examined in this chapter are different from all the APIs examined so far. Not only do they rely on the browser adopting the APIs, they rely on servers implementing these APIs as well, since they do not play well with most existing web servers or web infrastructure (such as firewalls and proxy servers).

This chapter will not provide working examples due to the fact it is not possible to provide simple server-side examples.

Server sent events

The first problem we will deal with is the server sending unsolicited notifications to the client. This is a very common problem in web applications, for instance, consider the Gmail application: it needs to alert users to the fact that a new email has been received.

It is not possible for the server to open a connection to a client to send it notifications. In order to achieve this, the client would need to act as a server, and open a port for the server to connect to. This would open up the client to major security vulnerabilities, and would be prohibited by firewalls.

Instead, the functionality can be achieved with polling. In the Gmail scenario, the client could send a message to the server every few seconds to ask if any new emails have arrived.

There are two main problems with polling:

1. It is very wasteful on network resources, since most of the time there will be no new emails. If we envisage a user receiving 2 emails an hour, polling ever 5 seconds would mean 359 requests informing the user there are no new emails for each 1 informing them there is a new email.

2. It involves latency, since it will take on average half the polling interval to notify the user of a new email. For instance, if we increased the polling period to every 10 seconds, it will take on average 5 seconds to inform the user a new email has arrived (excluding network latency).

Software engineers have attempted to solve these problems using a technique (or rather a set of techniques) referred to as COMET.

COMET is usually implemented by having the client poll the server with a standard HTTP request. If the server has a notification for the client it will return it immediately. If the server does not have a notification for the client it will block the connection on the server until a notification is available, at which point an HTTP response will be returned. This technique is also sometimes referred to as "long-polling".

There are problems with this approach that make it unattractive for most sites:

1. Due to the way most web servers implement connection management, while the request is blocked on the server it is represented by an open operating system thread. This significantly reduces the number of clients that can be supported by a single server, since there are limits to the number of active threads.

2. Many clients sit behind firewalls, and firewalls are often suspicious of connections that remain open for significant periods of time. In order to circumvent this COMET implementations usually only leave the request open for a limited period (perhaps 20 seconds). After this period, the request times out and a new request is sent from the client. This therefore reduces the latency for receiving notifications, but does not really reduce network traffic.

Essentially COMET is a hack. It is a set of techniques for implementing a common problem that lacks a good solution. The Server Sent Events API on the other hand is a solution to the underlying problem.

The Server Sent Events API is relatively simple from the point of view of the client. The browser indicates it wishes to receive server sent events by creating an Event Source, which in turn sends an HTTP request to the server. The HTTP request is sent to the URL specified in the EventSource: this must be a service capable of handling Server Sent Events:

```
var eventSource = new EventSource("/newtasks.php");
```

The server will respond to this HTTP request with an HTTP response with the MIME type of **text/event-stream**. The server can then begin using the connection to send messages to the client.

The client identifies the end of a message, and the start of a new one by two empty new lines in the payload, although this detail is hidden from you as a JavaScript programmer; instead a listener is attached to the event source to access the server sent events:

```
eventSource.onmessage = function(event) {

  console.log(event.data)

}
```

The data sent by server sent events is just plain text, encoded with the UTF-8 character encoding. The messages can of course conform to a data format standard such as XML or JSON, but this is not a requirement.

If it is so simple to implement server sent events you may be wondering why you have not heard more about them. Unfortunately server sent events suffer from the same problems as COMET:

1. Many web servers (including Apache) are not capable of leaving a connection open for an extended period of time (which Server Sent Events requires) without utilizing resources on the server. Many servers will need to change the way they perform connection management before they can effectively support Server Sent Events.

2. Many clients are behind firewalls which prevent connections being left open for an extended period of time.

A new class of server has begun to emerge designed specifically to work with this new paradigm; this is resolving the first of these problems. The most prominent amongst these servers is probably Node.js. Node.js utilizes JavaScript as its programming language, proving that JavaScript can live outside the browser.

Node.js is only a solution to this problem however if clients connect directly to it. Many IT infrastructures proxy all requests through a proxy server in a less secure area of their network (often referred to as the DMZ), and therefore the use of Server Sent Events could still cause issues if this proxy server was incapable of handling long-lived connections.

The second problem can be mitigated with error handling. If the underlying connection is closed by a firewall, an exception will be raised which the client can listen for:

```
eventSource.onerror = function(e) {

  console.log("EventSource error occurred");

};
```

When an error occurs, the EventSource can be re-established with the server.

Due to the fact that Server Sent Events are HTTP based, it is possible to provide Polyfills for browsers lacking support based on COMET techniques, but obviously these suffer from the same limitations as current COMET based techniques.

Web Sockets

As discussed above, Server Sent Events continue to utilize standard HTTP requests and responses, but allow the server (rather than the client) to initiate requests.

Web sockets on the other hand are an API for real-time, bi-directional communication between the client and server using a TCP based protocol. HTTP does use TCP as the underlying transport protocol, but HTTP is designed for larger payloads, and is not intended to be conversational.

Web Sockets are designed to allow the client and server to be as chatty with each other as they like by imposing minimal overhead on each message sent and received. In addition, Web Socket connections are full duplex: so it is possible to send and receive data simultaneously on the same connection.

Although Web Sockets uses a distinct protocol from HTTP, they do continue to use the same HTTP ports (typically 80 and 443). This ensures that additional ports do not need to be opened to use Web Sockets.

The initial handshake between the client and the server to establish the connection looks like a regular HTTP GET request, except it contains a request to upgrade the HTTP connection:

```
GET /tasklist HTTP/1.1

Host: testing.com

Upgrade: websocket

Connection: Upgrade

Sec-WebSocket-Key: f4JUFGdKI3ReHYt8JHETuo==

Sec-WebSocket-Protocol: chat

Sec-WebSocket-Version: 13
```

The server will then respond with an HTTP request, confirming that the HTTP connection has been upgraded to a Web Socket connection:

```
HTTP/1.1 101 Switching Protocols

Upgrade: websocket

Connection: Upgrade

Sec-WebSocket-Accept: HjGT6d6YJHyyERmm5HY5TreKjWk=

Sec-WebSocket-Protocol: chat
```

Once the connection has been established, either the client or the server are able to initiate the transfer of text data to the other party, and this communication will utilize the Web Socket (TCP based) protocol.

The complexity of the HTTP handshake is largely irrelevant from the programmers point of view. The following code will establish a Web Socket connection:

```
var connection = new WebSocket('ws://localhost/tasklist', ['json']);
```

Notice that the URL is not prefixed with HTTP:

```
ws://localhost/tasklist
```

This could also be set to "wss" in order to use a secure connection.

The second parameter contains a list of sub-protocols (or data formats) that the client accepts. This is used to ensure the client and the server are speaking the same language on top of the Web

Socket protocol. For instance, some applications may wish to use JSON data formats, while others will use XML, while the server may support both data formats. If multiple sub-protocols are specified, the server can determine the preferred protocol. It is even possible to utilize a custom protocol specific to the application you are writing.

It is possible to attach a callback to the connection to hear that the connection has been established:

```
connection.onopen = function () {
    console.log('The connection is open');
};
```

If the client specified that it accepted multiple protocols, it can also determine which one the server selected in the **onopen** method:

```
connection.onopen = function () {
  if (ws.protocol == 'json') {
    console.log('Json was selected');
  }
}
```

As soon as the connection is declared you can also add the usual callbacks to listen for messages or errors:

```
connection.onerror = function (error) {
  console.log('Error ' + error);
};
connection.onmessage = function (event) {
  console.log(event.data);
};
```

In addition, once the connection is established, the client can send messages to the server any time:

```
connection.send('this is a message');
```

Another major benefit of Web Sockets is that they can be used to perform cross-origin calls. As we have seen above, AJAX calls are limited by the same-origin policy: Web Sockets have no such restrictions. It is up to the server to determine if it will accept requests from all origins, or restrict requests to specific origins.

Web sockets are a young technology, and currently lack support in most web servers. In addition, despite the efforts made with the protocol, it may not work with proxy servers or firewalls. Node.js does however provide support for Web Sockets via various libraries. There are also servers available using Python, Ruby, PHP and Java.

It is likely to be a number of years before Web Sockets see widespread use, but it is a technology to watch. Once the implementation hurdles have been addressed, and common web servers begin to provide support, they are likely to see significant use.

17 ERROR HANDLING

Throughout this book we have developed a web application. There is one notable step that we have missed in this development however: a strategy for handling errors.

Errors can occur in a web application for many reasons, but it is worth subdividing errors into two categories:

1. Errors that can be anticipated. An example of this is an AJAX call that fails because the user is not connected to the Internet. We will call these exceptions, since they are exceptions to the rule.

2. Errors that are not anticipated. These errors normally arise from programming bugs, such as accessing an element in an array that does not exist, or accessing a property on an undefined object. We will call these errors, since they are errors in the implementation of the software rather than run-time conditions.

Detecting Errors

The first step in implementing an error handling strategy is detecting the fact that errors have occurred. The first type of error can be handled by the try/catch block within functions, or via registered callbacks on asynchronous APIs. All APIs that utilize asynchronous callbacks differentiate between success and failure scenarios, and we have also seen that jQuery **promises** provide direct support for this.

The second type of exception can be handled with try/catch blocks, but in general should not be. By definition, these errors should not occur, therefore you should prevent them from occurring rather than handling them.

For instance, consider a scenario where we have been passed an object that may be undefined, and we wish to access a property on it. We could write this as follows:

```
function accept(obj) {
    try {
    console.log(obj.property1);
    } catch (e){}
```

```
}
```

It is far better to write this as follows:

```
function accept(obj) {
    if (obj) {
        console.log(obj.property1);
    }
}
```

It is still important to know that unexpected errors have occurred, otherwise you will have no way of knowing your code contains a bug. Rather than adding try/catch blocks to all our functions, a more effective strategy for learning than an unanticipated error has occurred is by adding an **onerror** listener to the **window**:

```
window.onerror=function(message, url, lineNumber) {
    console.log('Message:'+message);
    console.log('URL:'+url);
    console.log('Line:'+lineNumber);
}
```

Add the following to the tasks.html page.

Now, we will add the following buggy function to the public section of tasks-controller.js:

```
printProperty: function(obj, property) {
    console.log(obj[property]);
}
```

Back in tasks.html, we are then going to call this after initialization:

```
tasksController.init($('#taskPage'), function() {
    tasksController.loadTasks();
    tasksController.printProperty(undefined, 'test');
});
```

If you run this example, you should see the following printed to the console:

```
Message:Uncaught TypeError: Cannot read property 'test' of undefined
URL:http://localhost:8080/scripts/tasks-controller.js
Line:123
▶ Uncaught TypeError: Cannot read property 'test' of undefined
>
```

Handling Errors

Now that we have detected errors, the next step is deciding what to do with them. It is important that you, as the application programmer, understand that these errors have occurred. Unlike with a server however, there is no centralized log file containing all the errors that have occurred.

In the case of exceptions, the requirements should specify what to do if an exception occurs. For instance, if an AJAX call cannot be performed:

Should the user be informed?

Should we try to carry on the best we can without the data from the AJAX call?

Should we prevent the user performing any other actions on the web page?

The answers to these questions depend on the requirements. Detecting the exception is the first step, but detection cannot help you determine what should be done with the exception.

When an error is detected there is not usually anything that can be done except document the fact that the error has occurred. Due to the fact that errors are unanticipated, they should not be handled by the code, but unless you document the fact they have occurred it is unlikely you will ever notice that they have occurred, since you cannot see a log of the users console.

My preferred approach for handling errors is to log them with the log4js library. A link to this library is provided in Appendix B. This library allows you to define a strategy for handling errors, which may include sending them to the server via AJAX so that they can be logged in a centralized file.

18 CONCLUSION

When assessing technology for new projects I like to apply a 10-year rule: "what will people think of this technology in 10 years time?"

- Will the software continue to function "as-is" on the devices commonly used in 10-years time?

- Will the software continue to function on existing devices, but need to be rewritten for new devices?

- Will the software need to be upgraded (and maybe rewritten) to continue its relevance?

- Will the software be obsolete and need to be discarded?

- Will anyone even remember this technology?

The 10-year horizon seems sensible for me. Vendors make a huge investment in the software they develop, and 10-years seems a reasonable period of time to expect software to at least remain relevant. In addition, vendors need to support and maintain their applications for extended periods of time, and this becomes challenging when technology becomes obsolete or "end-of-lifed".

There is no way to know for sure what the future holds for any technology. When Java was first introduced it was assumed Java Applets (applications that run inside browsers) would be a huge selling point for vendors, and would become a ubiquitous presence on the Internet. Although they can be found occasionally, Applets are all but obsolete, even as Java has gone from strength to strength as a server side language.

I firmly believe that the languages presented in this book will survive the 10-year rule. Web applications based on these languages may need to be modified to support new devices, but the underlying languages are in a strong position to maintain or strengthen their dominance. This chapter will examine the reasons I believe this.

History of backwards compatibility

HTML and JavaScript both have a tremendous track record when it comes to backwards compatibility. Web sites written in the late 1990's, relying on CGI scripts and early versions of HTML, still work largely unchanged. They typically do not look any better than they did in the 1990's, but they do still work.

Browser vendors take amazing care with backwards compatibility. They are aware that their users will hold them accountable if they ruin their browsing experience on a popular web site. As such, browser vendors invest huge resources in compatibility and regression testing every time a new release of a browser occurs.

This process is not perfect. As browser vendors have moved to faster and faster release cycles bugs do occasionally appear in existing web applications. Although this is an annoyance, at least it is possible for web application vendors to provide patches to their applications without requiring users to perform any upgrade steps.

Although bugs do sometimes appear therefore, the underlying APIs and feature sets remain remarkably stable once they are implemented in all major browsers.

As a result, web standards tend to be a process of extension rather than change, and this process looks set to continue. As mentioned earlier, HTML5 is considered a living standard, and will gradually change over time, without ever being replaced in a wholesale manner.

Monopoly Power

HTML and JavaScript are in a particularly strong position due to their monopoly position in the web browser, and the fact that web browsers exist for virtually all consumer computing devices (from phones, to games consoles, to tablets and laptops, to PCs).

Until recently Microsoft Windows held such a dominant position in operating systems that it made sense for vendors to produce applications that worked only in Microsoft Windows. Thanks to the explosion of hand-held devices, and the resurgence of Apple, this is no longer the case. Many people now use 2 or 3 distinct operating systems on a daily basis:

- A Microsoft Windows PC at work
- An Adnroid mobile phone
- An OSX laptop at home
- An iOS based iPad

Increasingly users expect to use the same applications across all these devices, and for data to be synchronized between the devices.

Web Applications written for web browsers offer enormous potentials in this area. Using the languages outlined in this book it is relatively trivial to write an application that runs on all these platforms, and performs synchronization to each device via a central server.

Ironically, unless any vendor establishes monopoly power over devices the way Microsoft did in the period from 1995-2005 it is unlikely that JavaScript and HTML will loose their monopoly. This is partly because the strengths of HTML5 and JavaScript, and partly because it is so difficult for multiple vendors to agree on a new set of technologies to replace them.

HTML as a Living Standard

Another reason I am confident in the future prospects of HTML5 is that it is a living standard. As we saw earlier in the book, even the HTML5 DOCTYPE does not have a version number associated with it. Web based technologies will continue to evolve over time, new standards will be released, and some older features may be deprecated. Despite this, the vast majority of HTML5 will still be in place in 10 years time, just as the vast majority of HTML4 is still supported.

Living standards do have their problems. Browser vendors will implement new standards according to their own timeframes, therefore the need for polyfills is unlikely to go anywhere anytime soon. The competition between browser vendors to support these features is ultimately good for browser technology however.

The evolution of web standards is likely to focus on adding more and more APIs that will ultimately make web applications as powerful as desktop applications.

Consider mobile phone applications: the vast majority of these are written for iPhone and Android using native SDKs. This is largely due to the fact that these provide APIs for features such as:

- Accessing the camera
- Using Bluetooth
- Accessing the phone book
- Accessing files
- Accessing the compass

Native SDKs represent a challenge to software engineers and companies producing commercial software however, since the same application needs to be written multiple times to support each SDK. In addition, applications need to be verified and possibly modified each time a new operating system is released.

Ideally mobile phones and tablets would present a unified development platform with a suite of APIs that were supported on all mobile operating systems.

It is likely HTML5 will grow over time to fill this desire. There is no reason that these features of mobile phones could not be supported in a cross platform JavaScript API, and made available inside the browser.

An interesting project began a few years ago called PhoneGap (the underlying software is now called Apache Cordoba). This allows applications to be written for a variety of mobile phone platforms using HTML5 features. Where features are not supported in HTML5 (such as Bluetooth), these are provided via a custom JavaScript library.

PhoneGap applications are packaged as native applications, but underneath they are using HTML, JavaScript and CSS.

The goal of PhoneGap is to make itself obsolete over time. This has already begun to happen with APIs such as the GeoLocation API now available natively inside browsers. The main obstacle that would need to be overcome to make PhoneGap obsolete is security. HTML based applications run inside the browser sandbox, and are not given access to the file-system and other aspects of the operating system.

Mobile phone applications also run inside a sandbox, and ask the user for permissions to perform restricted tasks. There is therefore no reason that web browsers could not adopt this same model, in fact some browsers already ask the user for permission before allowing usage of the storage APIs.

The End

I hope this book has convinced you not only the value and utility of HTML5, JavaScript and jQuery; but also their underlying beauty and elegance. The future is remarkably bright for these languages, and the software engineers who harness their power. I wish you all the best in your endeavors, and hope this book has provided the foundations you need to write your own web applications.

Again, I would love to hear your feedback. Please don't hesitate to contact me at dane@cisdal.com.

APPENDIX A: CSS

Up until this point we have not examined the manner in which HTML documents are styled within the browser. HTML itself should not contain presentational information (colors, fonts, borders etc), in fact most of the remaining presentational aspects of HTML have been removed in HTML5. Presentation of documents is left to the Cascading Style Sheets (CSS) style sheet language.

This provides a separation of concerns: the HTML page provides the content, while CSS provides the presentation information. This ensures that either can be changed independently of the other.

CSS3 is the latest version of the CSS specification, and is being progressed in parallel with the HTML5 specification.

This appendix will provide a brief introduction to layout with CSS, without focusing on the latest features added to CSS in CSS3, and without focusing on how individual elements can be styled. As such, this introduction is aimed at software engineers and programmers rather than designers.

There are four keys to understanding CSS to a level sufficient to layout complex pages.

The first aspect is to understand how elements are selected by CSS to have styles applied to them. As discussed earlier, jQuery uses the same selection syntax as CSS, therefore this should be intuitive to you even if you have not used CSS before.

The second is to understand the box model. This is the model that describes the rectangle that is rendered to represent each element in the document tree. If you look at the elements that compose an HTML document, each visible element is represented by a rectangle. When an element is a child of another element, its rectangle is inside its parent rectangle.

 This is slightly simplistic, rectangles can overlap other rectangles, and sit on top off, rather than inside, other rectangles, but we will use this simplistic model to begin.

The third is to understand how elements are positioned on screen, and how they interact with one another. There are several ways to position elements on screen, and several different ways elements of different type can interact with one another.

The forth is to understand the way styles do or don't inherit styles from their parents. For instance, if a **table** element has a background color of blue, should its **tr** and **td** children inherit this style? Some styles cascade, and some (for good reason) do not.

Selecting elements

CSS consists of a set of stylistic properties that should be applied to a set of elements. The following is an example of two properties being applied to all elements of type **footer**:

```
footer {
    font-size: 12px;
    text-align:center;
}
```

As with jQuery, you can specify rules for elements with specific classes:

```
.classname {

}
```

With specific IDs:

```
#idvalue {

}
```

Or with pseudo classes (the jQuery equivalent of filters):

```
a:visited {

}
```

As with jQuery, you can also combine multiple rules in the same selector. This will match all **td** elements inside a **table** with the ID **tblOne**:

```
#tblOne td {

}
```

While this will match all **td** elements that have the class **underlined**:

```
.underlined.td {

}
```

All matched elements will have the styles specified applied to them, and, as we will see below, these styles will sometimes be inherited by their children.

Elements can be styled by more than one set of rules. For instance, if we have a **footer** defined as follows:

```
<footer class="myfooter" id="footer1">
```

And the following rules:

```
footer {
```

```
    color:black;
}
.myfooter {
    background:blue;
}
# footer1 {
    font-size:12pt;
}
```

Then the footer will have all three styles applied to it:

```
font-size:12pt;
background:blue;
color:black;
```

This does not present a problem when the properties are unique, but what if the styles had been defined as follows?:

```
footer {
    color:black;
}
.myfooter {
    color:blue;
}
# footer1 {
    color:red;
}
```

In this case, CSS needs to find the most precise rule, and select the appropriate color based on that. There are several ways this is done.

Firstly, CSS uses a priority system to determine which rule has the most weight to it:

• If a match is based on element type, the rule is assigned 1 point.

• If it matches on class, the rule is assigned 10 points.

• If it matches on ID, the rule is assigned 100 points.

This means that a match against the following rule will be assigned 11 points (it has one element match, and one class match):

```
footer .myclass
```

The rule with the highest score wins. This means that in our case, the color selected would be red, since the ID based rule is awarded 100 points. This process is referred to as "specificity".

This is already getting complex, but unfortunately it gets even more complex.

Rules can be specified in 3 different ways:

1. We can create an external CSS file, and import it into the HTML file.

2. We can create styles "inline" in the HTML document by placing them between <style></style> tags.

3. We can specify styles directly on an element, for instance, <footer style="color:blue;font-size:12pt">

Any styles assigned specifically on the element are awarded an extra 1000 points, meaning they will almost always override any other styles.

Even after applying all these rules, it is possible that two rules will have the same specificity. In this case, the one defined last will win. This means that rules inside <style></style> blocks override those defined in external CSS files, and if multiple rules in the same CSS file have the same specificity, the last rule, in the last file listed is the winner.

Finally, if you are unable to increase the specificity of a rule sufficiently to trump another rule, but have one or more styles that should never be overridden, you can use the **!important** flag. When this is used only inline styles will be able to override the style:

```
.myfooter {
    color:blue !important;
}
```

In general it is best not to have to rely on this setting.

The Box Model

The box model dictates the area that an element takes up on screen, and therefore impacts the positioning of other elements that need to be positioned around it.

Each element in the document tree is represented on screen by a rectangular box. This includes **div** elements, **span** elements, **a** elements, and any other element in the document tree that has a visual aspect.

In order to understand CSS layout it is necessary to understand the various stylistic properties that affect the size of a box.

• Firstly, each box needs an area where its content should appear.

• Secondly, you may specify padding between the content and the border.

• Thirdly, you may specify the size of the border.

• And fourthly, you can specify the margin that should occur between the border of this component and the components positioned adjacent to it.

In addition, you need to consider what it means to set the background color of the element: should that fill the entire space, just the content, or something in between?

These four properties constitute the box model that can be seen in the diagram below:

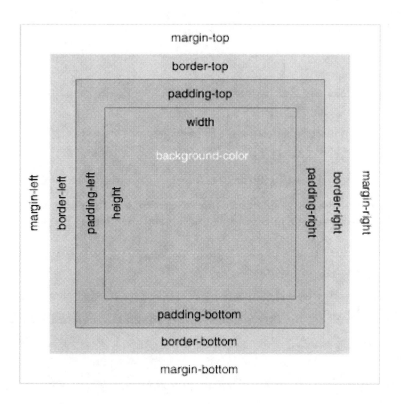

The **height** and **width** properties applied to the element dictate the content size, while the combination of padding, border and margin around this dictate the overall size of the box on screen.

As can be seen, the background color fills the content and padding portions of the box. The border will typically have its own color, while the margin will inherit the background color of the element's parent.

All of these aspects of the box model can be controlled by CSS. For instance, consider the following set of properties:

```
.element {
border: 1px solid #AAA;
padding: 10 0 10 0px;
margin-right: 15px;
width: 200px;
height: 100px;
}
```

In this example, the content of the element will consume a total of 200x100px.

The padding has then been declared as a single property with 4 values (rather than as padding-left, padding-right etc). This is applying 10px to the top and bottom, and 0 to the left and right. The way to remember the order of the 4 values is TRouBLe (Top, Right, Bottom, Left).

One more pixel is then being added for the border, and 15 pixels of margin to the right of the element.

This means that the height of the element will be 100+10+10+1+1 = 122px, while the width will be 200+1+1+15=217px.

It is worth mentioning that the margin set on an element can be negative. This causes an element to take up less space than it otherwise would.

Positioning Elements

In order to fully understand the position an element will take on screen, and the way it interacts with adjacent elements, it is also necessary to take into account the value of the **display** property.

This can be one of 4 primary values:

• **inline**: this is the default for **span**, **a** and **td** elements.

• **block**: this is the default for most other elements, including **div**, **p** and most other elements.

• **inline-block**: this is only the default for the **img** element, but is commonly assigned to other elements in CSS.

• **none**: the element should be hidden from view.

It is possible to override the **display** property of any elements as follows:

```
.myclass {
    display:inline-block;
}
```

The primary difference between these display types is as follows:

• An inline element does not have a line break either before or after it, and can sit vertically adjacent to other elements. In addition, you cannot set the height or width properties for an inline element, although you can set **line-height** (this property dictates' the distance from the top of the first line of text to the top of the second).

• An inline-block element is like an inline element in that it doesn't force a line break (so elements can sit vertically adjacent to other elements), but it can be assigned **height** and **width**.

• A block element forces a new line before and after the element, therefore, by default, two block elements cannot sit vertically adjacent to each other.

• An element set to the display value of **none** does not take up any space on screen, not even the space it would take up if it was made visible.

The default display type of elements is not always appropriate when laying out the screen. Consider a screen with the following layout:

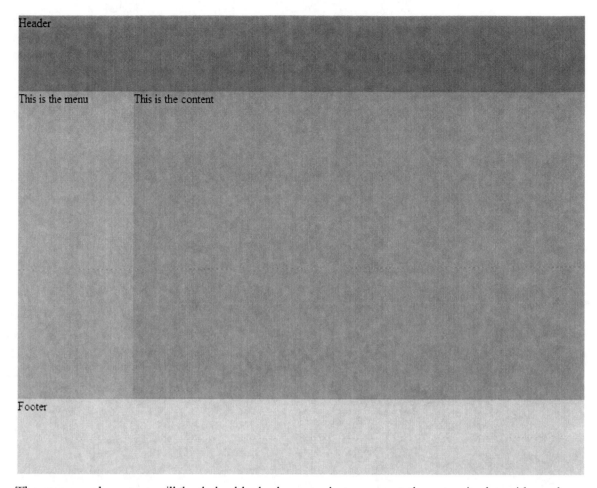

The menu and content will both be block elements, but we want them to sit alongside each other. In order to achieve that we can use the float property: this tells an element to float to the left or right of the preceding element, instead of above or below the element.

The following is the sample code to produce the desired results:

```
<!DOCTYPE html>
<html>
<head>
<style>
header {
    height:100px;
    background: blue;
}
.menu {
    float:left;
```

```
    width:20%;
    height:400px;
    background: red;
}
.content {
    float:right;
    height:400px;
    width:80%;
    background: green;
}
footer {
    clear:both;
    height: 100px;
    background: orange;
}
</style>
</head>
<body>
<header>
Header
</header>
<div class="menu">
This is the menu
</div>
<div class="content">
This is the content
</div>
<footer>
Footer
</footer>
</body>
</html>
```

The header is a **header** element, which is of type **display:block**. This means that by default it takes up 100% of the width and creates a new line after it. Therefore we only need to set the **height**.

The menu and content need to sit alongside each other; in order to achieve this, we set the menu to **float:left**, and the content to **float:right**, and assign them each a percentage of the overall width.

You may now think that the footer element only needs to be given a **height** (as per the header element). In fact, once we start floating elements, the page will keep floating block elements until it is told to stop, therefore we need to add the **clear:both** property (**both** refers to left and right, they can be cleared independently).

This simple example shows a lot of what you need to know in order to layout elements on screen.

We could have achieved a similar result by setting menu and content display to inline-block, but the disadvantage would be that the content would wrap to the next line if it did not fit beside menu.

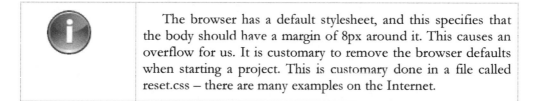

> The browser has a default stylesheet, and this specifies that the body should have a margin of 8px around it. This causes an overflow for us. It is customary to remove the browser defaults when starting a project. This is customary done in a file called reset.css – there are many examples on the Internet.

By now it should be relatively obvious how to position elements on screen when they are positioned via their interactions with other elements. This is called static positioning.

It is possible to specify element positioning as relative:

```
postion:relative
```

By itself this does absolutely nothing, but it makes it possible to move an element with the **left**, **right**, **top** and **bottom** properties, and move it from the position it would otherwise hold in the flow.

It is also possible to use absolute positioning. This removes the element from the main flow of elements, and places it explicitly at the position specified with the **left**, **right**, **top**, **bottom** properties. Absolutely positioned elements do not interact with other elements on the page: they can sit on top of or behind other elements. In order to control which element is on top, the **z-index** property can be used: the element with the highest **z-index** is positioned on top of the other elements.

The final type of positioning is fixed:

```
position:fixed
```

This can be used to fix elements in the browser even when the main page is scrolled. This is not a particularly common mode, but does have its uses.

Inheritance

The final fundamental aspect to understanding CSS is understanding when styles from the parent are inherited by their children and when they are not. For instance, consider the following HTML:

```
<div>
```

```
<span>this is text</span>
<span>this is more text</span>
</div>
```

If we apply a style to the **div**, it may or may not make sense to apply that style to the **span** elements. For instance, it does make sense to cascade the font, since it is a reasonable assumption that parents and children will use the same fonts. This means we can set a font for the body of the document, and automatically have it apply to all elements unless it is overridden.

Consider the case of a border though. If we were to specify a border for the **div**, we would not want this to cascade to the **span**, since that would cause a border to be rendered around the **span** elements. Likewise, positioning and spacing styles such as padding, margin, top and left are not inherited.

There are some styles where it is dubious whether they should be inherited. Background color is an example: this does not get inherited, although there are many cases where this would make sense. It is however possible for a child to inherit this if it wants using:

```
background-color: inherit;
```

Debugging

Chrome makes it relatively simple to debug elements, and dynamically add styles. It is possible to right click on any element and select "Inspect Element". This will load the element into the "Elements" tab of the developer tools, and show the CSS properties that have been applied to the element.

```
▶ Computed Style              ☐ Show inherited
▼ Styles                      +  ⬚  ⚙-
element.style {
}
```

```
Matched CSS Rules
media="screen"                    tasks.htm
td {                              tasks.css:6
  ☑ font-size: 11px;
  ☑ line-height: 25px;
  ☑ padding-left: 10px;
}

media="screen"                    tasks.htm
table, th, td {                   tasks.css:3
  border: ▶1px solid ▇#888;
}

media="screen"                    tasks.htm
body, h1, h2, h3, h4,             tasks.css:
h5, h6, p, ul, dl, ol, form,
fieldset, input, label, table,
tbody, tfoot, th, tr, td, textarea,
select {
  font-family: "helvetica neue",
      helvetica, "lucinda sans
      unicode", "sans serif";
  font-weight: normal;
  color: ▇#333;
  padding: ▶0;
  border: ▶0;
  margin: ▶0;
  font-size: 12px;
}
```

Any styles that have been overridden are shown with a line through them, indicating they ae having no impact on the visual styling of the element.

It is also possible to dynamically add CSS properties in the top section of this window, allowing you to try out possibilities in real time.

Conclusion

The goal of this chapter is to teach you the fundamentals of CSS. Like many of the other web languages in this book, CSS appears simple, but without understanding the fundamentals it can be enormously frustrating.

APPENDIX B: RECOMMENDED LIBRARIES

This chapter will provide a brief introduction to some of the JavaScript libraries I have found useful when developing web applications.

Underscore

If you ever find yourself asking "why doesn't JavaScript have a function to do x?", chances are it will exist in the Underscore library. Underscore contains a wide array of utility functions for managing arrays, objects and functions, along with templating functionality similar to that used with jQuery Template.

The library, along with its API can be found here:

http://underscorejs.org/

jQuery UI

jQuery UI contains a wide range of UI widgets, ranging from progress bars, to dialogs, to drag and drop based lists. The library itself is reasonably large, but the capabilities of the widgets are extensive.

It is also possible to selectively include widgets from the library in your applications.

The project can be found here:

http://jqueryui.com/

Datatable

One important widget not included in jQuery UI is a table. It is common for web applications to require tables supporting of sorting, filtering and pagination.

The Datatable library provides a wrapper over top of regular HTML tables, and converts them into the rich and dynamic tables programmers are used to in desktop GUI toolkits:

https://datatables.net/

D3

D3 is a library for producing data driven documents. Charts and graphs are examples of data driven documents, but D3 can produce data bound documents of amazing complexity and elegance.

A full set of demos can be found at the project home page:

http://d3js.org/

Log4j JS

This library provides a logging API for JavaScript similar to the log4j (and related) library popular with Java. This API allows you to write custom appenders to dictate logging strategies, and provides an AJAX appender to send logs to the server: http://log4js.berlios.de/

CPSIA information can be obtained at www.ICGtesting.com
Printed in the USA
LVOW09s2007290515

440457LV00018B/662/P